**God's Word on Human Sexuality:
It's not what many think!**

God's Word on Human Sexuality:

It's not what many think!

by
David A. Palmer

PLACE TO GROW
PRESS

2019

Some scripture quotations from The Authorized (King James) Version. Rights in the Authorized Version in the United Kingdom are vested in the Crown. Reproduced by permission of the Crown's patentee, Cambridge University Press

Some scripture quotations are from the New Revised Standard Version Bible, copyright © 1989 the Division of Christian Education of the National Council of the Churches of Christ in the United States of America. Used by permission. All rights reserved.

Scripture taken from the Holy Bible, NEW INTERNATIONAL VERSION®, NIV® Copyright © 1973, 1978, 1984, 2011 by Biblica, Inc.® Used by permission. All rights reserved worldwide.

Copyright © 2019 by Dr. David A. Palmer All rights reserved.

This book or any portion thereof may not be reproduced or used in any manner whatsoever without the express written permission of the publisher except for the use of brief quotations in a book review or scholarly journal.

Printed in the United States of America

First Printing, 2019

ISBN 978-1-7321245-6-1

Place to Grow Press
1435 East Main Street
Kent, OH 44240
www.KentMethodist.org

CONTENTS

Prologue vii

The Witness of the Whole Bible 1

Sodom and Gomorrah 7

A Parallel to the Story of Sodom. 17

Homosexuality in Biblical Times 23
    The Old Testament Context

Selective Literalism and the
Laws of Leviticus 35

Why Would Laws in Leviticus
No Longer Apply? 47

Homosexuality in Biblical Times 53
    The New Testament Context

The Homosexual Behavior Condemned
by Paul 59

Is Same-Sex Activity Unnatural and
to Be Judged? 69

Strange Flesh 81

What God Creates Is Good 85

Is Celibacy the Christian Rule for
LGBTQ Persons?. 91

Marriage in the Biblical Understanding. 95

The Welcome of Jesus and the Dynamic of
"Welcoming the Sinner, Not the Sin" 105

The Church's Welcome 111

The Church's Outreach 119

Moving Past Accommodation to Culture. 125

The Authority of Scripture. 129

Epilogue 133

Prologue

The greatest debate in Christian churches today is on the subject of human sexuality. A prime example of disagreement among Christians was the 2019 General Conference of the United Methodist Church, which was entirely devoted to the church's stance on "the practice of homosexuality." The Conference resulted in a very split decision, as a narrow majority of 53% of delegates voted to uphold the stance that "the United Methodist Church does not condone the practice of homosexuality and considers this practice incompatible with Christian teaching." (from the United Methodist *Discipline*)

Notably, delegates on both sides of the issue appealed to the Bible, which means there must be some considerable confusion about Scriptural teaching in this regard! What exactly does the Bible say on the subject? Answering that question will be the aim of this book. The coming chapters will examine every passage in the Bible that refers in any way to sexual orientation or same-sex relationships. The guiding principle will be II Timothy 2:15—"Make every effort to present yourself before God as one approved, a worker who has no need to be ashamed, rightly explaining the word of truth." (Σπούδασον σεαυτὸν δόκιμον παραστῆσαι τῷ Θεῷ ἐργάτην ἀνεπαίσχυντον ὀρθοτομοῦντα τὸν λόγον τῆς ἀληθείας)

The first word in that verse, *spoudason*, meaning "make every effort," suggests that in order to rightly comprehend God's truth, one must do much more than a quick and superficial reading of the Bible! Too often people assume that the

Bible means whatever it seems to them at first glance to say. To "rightly explain the word of truth" requires an in-depth journey; and the following chapters will carefully examine the background, the context, and the precise meaning of each verse.

The results may be surprising to some. A particular challenge for Biblical study is the fact that everyone comes to the Bible with a large set of assumptions. People have long-standing ideas about what they think the Bible says—ideas that may be quite mistaken! In the seventeenth century, many church leaders were quite convinced that the Bible proclaims the earth to be the center of the universe, with the sun revolving around it. After all, Psalm 104:5 says, "The Lord set the earth on its foundations; it shall never be moved"; and Ecclesiastes 1:5 says, "The sun rises and goes down and hurries to the place where it rises." Moreover, it certainly looks as though the sun revolves around the earth! On this basis, the Catholic Church condemned the teaching of Galileo. Today it seems obvious to everyone that Biblical verses about the sun rising and going down are to be understood in a figurative way; and the attitude of the seventeenth century Catholic church is broadly condemned, since the church's simplemindedness not only hurt Galileo (who spent the rest of his days under house arrest) but spurred a rift between the Bible and science that continues to this day. Will some long-standing attitudes of today's church be likewise condemned in the future?

When I was a child, my parents took me to visit the National Cathedral in Washington, D.C. I was wearing my new sunglasses, which I did not want to take off. As we walked through the cathedral, I repeatedly remarked, "It's dark in here." "Take off your sunglasses!" they said. But I refused. It sure was dark in that place.

People universally tend to look at the Bible through a certain set of lenses. The Biblical word is refracted through the social attitudes and cultural values that people have picked up from their upbringing and their society. Typically, people do not realize how their understanding of the Bible is being distorted by the "cultural lenses" that they are wearing. A classic and tragic historical example of this was the way in which many American Christians used the Bible to support slavery. How did they manage to think that the Bible supported slavery, when the central Old Testament story is a saga of God delivering people *out* of slavery? Their distorted reading of the Bible occurred because they were reading the Bible through the lens of a slaving culture, with the result that they readily turned selected Biblical verses into supports for their own traditional practices. The consequences were horrendous for countless African slaves.

There is an old hymn about the Bible, long popular in many congregations, in which the refrain is, "Beautiful words, wonderful words, wonderful words of life." The Scriptures *are* words of life, but not when they are misread and misused!

Distorted readings of the Bible have continued into the present day. It was not many years ago that Christians in America were using the Bible to argue for segregation and to argue against interracial marriage, on the basis of the Genesis teaching that God had created everything, "each according to its own kind." (Genesis 1:24) This was taken to mean that whites and blacks were created by God with the intention that they would stay among "their own kind." The lens of a racist culture produced a very distorted understanding of the Biblical Word.

On questions of human sexuality, people approach the Bible within a long history of traditional ideas. People have long assumed that the Bible teaches that "the practice of homosexuality is incompatible with Christian teaching"—exactly what the United Methodist *Discipline* has stated—and they naturally read the Bible through the lens of that assumption. They may very well not realize that they are looking at the Bible through a set of culturally supplied lenses; after all, we often forget that we are wearing a pair of glasses! In order to truly see the Biblical Word, one must be willing to take off the lenses, in order to perceive the Bible in a new and unbiased light. Only then will the contemporary student of the Bible be able to "rightly explain the word of truth."

The Witness of the Whole Bible

All Scripture is inspired by God and is useful for teaching, for reproof, for correction, and for training in righteousness, so that everyone who belongs to God may be proficient, equipped for every good work.

II Timothy 3:16–17

Chapter 1

When the second letter to Timothy says that *all Scripture* is inspired by God, it points to the unity and integrity of the Bible. As diverse as the Bible is—with its sixty-six books written and shaped across many centuries by countless people—the whole Biblical message hangs together in a marvelous way. To rightly understand any verse of the Bible, one needs to read the verse in light of the whole.

The quickest way to misread the Bible is to lift up particular verses without regard to their context or their place in the overarching Biblical story. A classic example is the verse, "An eye for an eye and a tooth for a tooth" (Exodus 21:24), which is routinely cited by people as supposed example of brutally retributive justice. In fact, the "eye for an eye" law, in its original setting, was a *limitation* on retribution, as the law was put forth in a time when people were inclined to take excessive vengeance. That context is spelled out dramatically in the story of Lamech in the book of Genesis, in which Lamech, who typified the violence of ancient societies, declared that if anyone should wrong him, he would avenge himself by doing something seventy-seven times worse to that person. (Genesis 4:24) The dictum, "An eye for an eye and a tooth for a tooth" was a clear reversal of that kind of limitless vengeance, as it declared, "You shall take no more than a tooth for a tooth!" Jesus continued that movement away from vengeance, as he called people to *forgive* others seventy-seven times (Matthew 18:22)—thus surpassing the "eye for an eye" principle with a call for unlimited mercy. Obviously, the "eye for an eye" verse can only be rightly understood when it is seen in the context of the entire Biblical Word!

When it comes to verses about human sexuality, it is commonly the case that individual verses will be quoted without reference to their context or their place in the overall Biblical message. This can only result in severe misunderstanding.

To rightly comprehend God's Word, one must begin by looking at the whole Biblical story.

What does one find when one looks for what the entire Bible says about "the practice of homosexuality"? The most striking discovery that one initially makes when pursuing this question is that the Bible says *almost nothing.*

Look, for example, at the Biblical prophets, who have a great deal to say about how human beings are to live rightly in God's sight. The Bible contains the books of three major prophets—Isaiah, Jeremiah, and Ezekiel—and twelve "minor prophets." These prophets speak again and again at great length about important moral issues. There is not a single word expressing concern about same-sex relationships anywhere in the prophets.

Look through the wisdom writings—Psalms, Proverbs, Ecclesiastes, Job, or the Song of Solomon—which give much guidance on all sorts of subjects. There is nothing at all about "the practice of homosexuality." Look through the historical books of Samuel, Kings, Chronicles, Ezra, or Nehemiah. In the books of I and II Kings, there are several references to "male temple prostitutes," and this practice is thoroughly condemned. But the condemnation here is on cultic prostitution, not on homosexuality. The practice of cultic prostitution, and its implications for Biblical statements about homosexuality, will be discussed in a later chapter. But outside of cultic prostitution, there are no statements in the books of Samuel, Kings, Chronicles, Ezra, or Nehemiah about any kind of same-sex behavior.

If you look at the earliest books in the Bible, you do find, in the book of Genesis, the story of Sodom and Gomorrah, which often comes to mind when people think of homosexual practice. In fact, however, the Bible is quite clear that the practice of homosexuality was *not* the "grave sin" (Genesis 18:20) which brought God's judgment upon those cities. The Sodom and Gomorrah story will be explored in depth in the next chapter.

There is also a story in the book of Judges about a group of men who wanted to rape a male visitor to the town. (Judges 19) They ended up raping the man's concubine—an act thoroughly condemned in the Bible. The sin here was not homosexuality but rape.

Finally, in the book of Leviticus, in a section called the "Holiness Code," there are two verses that speak directly about the practice of homosexuality, in Leviticus 18:22 and 20:13. These two verses are both quite negative, but what is most striking about them—in the context of the entire Old Testament—is how unusual they are. The 39 books of the Old Testament contain a total of 23,145 verses. Just *two* of those verses are legal injunctions against some kind of practice of homosexuality. A future chapter will explore the historical setting and precise meaning of those two verses.

It is a general rule in the Bible that Old Testament trajectories come to their fulfillment in Jesus; and this again is very true on this subject. What did Jesus say about the practice of homosexuality? Absolutely nothing. For those who believe that Jesus is the ultimate revelation of God's Truth, there is a message here. If Jesus never spoke about the issue, it raises the very strong question as to whether there is actually a moral issue here in God's sight.

At the same time, there are a few references to same-sex practices in New Testament letters. There are three places in the New Testament—in I Corinthians, I Timothy, and Romans—where there is a reference, generally negative, to some sort of same-sex practice. Each of these references has its own unique context and vocabulary, so it will be very important to examine these verses in detail, so as to be clear about their actual meaning. But again, what is striking in the New Testament is the same as what was notable in the Old—these verses are rare. The New Testament has 27 books containing 7,957 verses. When just three short passages make a reference to same-sex practices, it is clear that this is not a major issue in the Bible.

Why therefore is this such a major issue in the church today? It is interesting that there is enormous uproar in churches today over a subject that scarcely receives mention in the Bible. The issue, of course, is that churches in the past adopted statements and policies against same-sex practices; and those statements and policies are now being challenged. In the United Methodist Church, the statement that "the practice of homosexuality is incompatible with Christian teaching" was inserted into the *Discipline*, the church's rule book, in 1972. But was that statement grounded in Biblical teaching, or was it more a reflection of cultural attitudes that held sway in the church at the time?

The following chapters will explore what the Bible actually teaches, looking at the specific verses that mention same-sex practices, examining their larger context, and looking as well at the overarching themes of the Biblical story that shed light on what Christian attitudes should be. This exploration will be grounded in the affirmation of II Timothy 3:16—*that all Scripture is inspired by God, and is suitable to teaching, for reproof, for correction, and for training in righteousness.* This verse declares that the Bible has authority, and that God is speaking through all the Scriptures to rightly guide Christians in life. What this means, quite plainly, is that believers are not to briefly read a few isolated passages in order to form an opinion; they are summoned to genuinely pay attention to the entire Bible, and to study the Bible in depth. Only with serious Bible study can Christians be rightly equipped for discipleship in the present age.

Sodom and Gomorrah

The two angels came to Sodom in the evening, and Lot was sitting in the gateway of Sodom. When Lot saw them, he rose to meet them, and bowed down with his face to the ground. He said, "Please, my lords, turn aside to your servant's house and spend the night, and wash your feet; then you can rise early and go on your way." They said, "No; we will spend the night in the square." But he urged them strongly; so they turned aside to him and entered his house; and he made them a feast, and baked unleavened bread, and they ate. But before they lay down, the men of the city, the men of Sodom, both young and old, all the people to the last man, surrounded the house; and they called to Lot, "Where are the men who came to you tonight? Bring them out to us, so that we may know them." Lot went out of the door to the men, shut the door after him, and said, "I beg you, my brothers, do not act so wickedly. Look, I have two daughters who have not known a man; let me bring them out to you, and do to them as you please; only do nothing to these men, for they have come under the shelter of my roof." But they replied, "Stand back!" And they said, "This fellow came here as an alien, and he would play the judge! Now we will deal worse with you than with them." Then they pressed hard against the man Lot, and came near the door to break it down. But the men inside reached out their hands and brought Lot into the house with them, and shut the door. And they struck with blindness the men who were at the door of the house, both small and great, so that they were unable to find the door.

Then the men said to Lot, "Have you anyone else here? Sons-in-law, sons, daughters, or anyone you have in the city—bring them out of the place. For we are about to destroy this place, because the outcry against its people has become great before the Lord, and the Lord has sent us to destroy it." So Lot went out and said to his sons-in-law, who were to marry his daughters, "Up, get out of this place; for the Lord is about to destroy the city." But he seemed to his sons-in-law to be jesting. When morning dawned, the angels urged Lot, saying, "Get up, take your wife and your two daughters who are here, or else you will be consumed in the punishment of the city." But he lingered; so the men seized him and his wife and his two daughters by the hand, the Lord being merciful to him, and they brought him out and left him outside the city.

Genesis 19:1–16

Chapter 2

When people think of a Biblical story that contains homosexuality, they typically think of Sodom and Gomorrah. Yet this is a prime example of a story in the Bible of which many people have heard but few people truly understand.

People commonly know that Sodom and Gomorrah were two ancient cities so sinful that God sent fire and brimstone in judgment upon them. The sinfulness of the cities is expressed in Genesis 18 when God declares to Abraham, "How very grave is the sin of Sodom and Gomorrah!" (Genesis 18:20) In the book of Genesis, however, it is never said what exactly the sin was.

The cities of Sodom and Gomorrah are first mentioned in Genesis 13, where there is a description of how Abraham (then called Abram) and his nephew Lot journeyed into the Promised Land. They decided to split into separate directions, and Abraham gave Lot the choice as to where he wished go. Lot decided to settle in Sodom. This is the first clue that Sodom was probably not a place of raging debauchery, even though it is depicted that way in many retellings of the story.

Further mention of Sodom and Gomorrah appears in Genesis 14, which describes a battle between multiple ancient cities, in which Sodom and Gomorrah are losers, but Abraham intercedes and routs their opponents. The chapter ends with the king of Sodom honoring Abraham. Sodom appears here as an ally of Abraham, and there is still no mention of wickedness in the city.

It is later, in Genesis 18, that God reveals to Abraham that God is about to bring judgment upon the cities of Sodom and Gomorrah because of "grave sin" in those cities. This sets up the famous account in Genesis chapter 19.

The chapter begins by saying that "two angels came to Sodom in the evening." (Genesis 19:1) In the Old Testament, angels appear on multiple occasions, and whenever they do, they typically look just like people. In this case, they are in male form. Genesis goes on to say that "Lot was sitting in the gateway of Sodom." (Genesis 19:1) This is where the men would gather in ancient days if they wanted to chat with people.

At this juncture, it is extremely important to understand that in the ancient near east, during this time period, one of the highest moral values was the value of hospitality. In an age when people were traveling without benefit of hotels and restaurants, travelers were very dependent on finding people who would welcome them in, to offer them food or lodging or both. The righteous person would show such hospitality and would readily welcome complete strangers, providing them with a meal and shelter for the night. Earlier in the book of Genesis, there is a story of Abraham showing precisely such hospitality to three angels (who again looked like ordinary people) who showed up at his tent. Abraham urged them to stop and rest; and he gave them a bountiful meal. (Genesis 18:1–8)

Once such guests came under a person's care, the truly righteous person would take responsibility for their well-being, for as long as they remained under one's roof. It is much as you would treat guests today. If someone is staying at your house, you want to be sure that they have everything that they need. In ancient days, which were dangerous times, when travelers could easily be robbed or assaulted, this care for the well-being of the guest went yet further. The righteous person would defend guests against any threat and would bar the door or take up arms against anyone who was trying to do harm to the guests. In fact, so sacred was the obligation to protect one's guests that the truly righteous person would be willing to make personal sacrifice, even perhaps sacrificing members of one's own family, for the sake of one's guests. All this will play out in the story of Lot.

As the angels approached Sodom, Genesis reports that "when Lot saw them, he rose to meet them, and bowed down with his face to the ground." He said, 'Please, my lords, turn aside to your servant's house and spend the night, and wash your feet; then you can rise early and go on your way.' They said, 'No; we will spend the night in the square.' But he urged them strongly; so they turned aside to him and entered his house; and he made them a feast, and baked unleavened bread, and they ate." (Genesis 19:1–3) Here Lot appears as the quintessentially righteous person, who graciously welcomes the guests and shows them magnanimous hospitality.

But the strangers receive a somewhat different welcome from the other townsfolk. The story continues, "But before they lay down, the men of the city, the men of Sodom, both young and old, all the people to the last man, surrounded the house; and they called to Lot, "Where are the men who came to you tonight? Bring them out to us, so that we may know them." (Genesis 19:4–5) This does not mean that the townspeople wanted to "get to know them." This Hebrew word translated "know" at this juncture meant "to have sexual intercourse" with them. In other words, the townspeople wanted to rape them.

When strangers come to town, the good person will receive them with gracious hospitality. When these two guys come to town, the men of Sodom want to gang rape them. You cannot get much worse than that. This of course would have been homosexual rape; but it would have been just as bad if the angels had been in female form and it had been heterosexual rape. The element of homosexuality is incidental to the story. The sin here was the sin of showing violent abuse rather than kindness to the stranger, and it demonstrated just how far the people of Sodom had turned from God.

The story continues and says, "Lot went out of the door to the men, shut the door after him, and said, "I beg you, my brothers, do not act so wickedly." (Genesis 19:6–7) There is the righteous man, barring the door, interceding to defend his guests. He apparently sensed that this initial entreaty was not working, so he continued and said, "Look, I have two daughters who have not known a man; let me bring them out to you, and do to them as you please; only do nothing to these men, for they have come under the shelter of my roof." (Genesis 19:8) When people today read this story, they are often aghast and perplexed at this point, thinking, "What is he doing!? He is offering to give his own daughters to this lecherous mob!" But keep in mind the ancient high value of hospitality—the truly righteous person would sacrifice even his own family for the sake of the guests. Lot is willing to make the ultimate sacrifice—his own children—for the sake of the strangers. Notice the foreshadowing of what happens in the New Testament, when God sends His Son Jesus to offer his life for the sake of strangers—namely, the whole of humanity.

But the men of the city will have none of it. The story continues: But they replied, "Stand back!" And they said, "This fellow [Lot] came here as an alien, and he would play the judge! Now we will deal worse with you than with them." Then they pressed hard against the man Lot, and came near the door to break it down. But the men inside [the angels] reached out their hands and brought Lot into the house with them, and shut the door." (Genesis 19:9–10) Lot is rescued by the angels he was standing to defend. The story continues with the men at the door being struck by blindness, and their efforts are foiled. Under the angels' instruction, Lot then gathers up his family to flee the city. But they hesitate, because they think it is really not so bad, and cannot believe that judgment is coming. Here again is a clue that the sinfulness of Sodom, for which the city was being judged, was not some sort of glaring wickedness.

Finally, the angels literally drag the family out of the city. The story concludes with the destruction of Sodom and Gomorrah as a consequence of the horrendous sin of the people.

But what exactly was the sin of Sodom and Gomorrah, which brought such judgment? God was already angered at the cities long before the incident involving attempted gang rape. The fact that the townspeople wanted to rape the visitors instead of welcoming them illustrated the depth of their moral corruption; but this does not tell us what had so outraged God about the cities in the first place. Later in the Bible, however, in the prophets, it is made very clear what exactly the sinfulness of Sodom was, which had moved the Lord to such disgust that God had decreed judgment. The prophet Ezekiel declared it as follows: "This was the sin of Sodom: she had pride, excess of food and prosperous ease, but did not aid the poor and needy." (Ezekiel 16:49) Those exact same sins are associated with Sodom in the prophets Isaiah and Jeremiah—pride, self-indulgence, and indifference to the needy.

According to the Bible, the sin of Sodom had nothing to do with same-sex relations, and everything to do with self-centeredness. This relates to a major theme in the prophets, who say nothing at all about same-sex relationships, but who continually speak about the moral problem of people who are focused on themselves and are unconcerned about the troubles of the world around them. All this has major implications for the present day. If the sin of Sodom was "pride, excess of food, and prosperous ease," along with a lack of caring for the poor and needy, it is apparent that the sin of Sodom is being widely repeated today—only not in the way that people think.

It is significant that in rabbinic commentary on the story of Sodom and Gomorrah, all the way up to the first century AD, there was never an association of those stories with homosexuality. It was only in the first century that Philo of Alexandria, a Jewish philosopher, suggested that the Sodom and Gomorrah sagas were concerned with the practice of homosexuality. Such a connection was *not* made, however, by the most important contemporary of Philo—Jesus.

Jesus referred explicitly to Sodom and Gomorrah, and when he did so, it was with clear reference to *hospitality*. When sending his disciples out to villages all around, Jesus instructed them as follows: "Whatever town or village you enter, search there for some worthy person and stay at their house until you leave. As you enter the home, give it your greeting... but if no one will welcome you or listen to your words, leave that place and shake the dust off your feet. Truly I tell you, it will be more bearable for Sodom and Gomorrah on the day of judgment than for that town." (Matthew 10:11–15) A parallel story is found in the gospel of Luke, where Jesus says the same thing. (Luke 10:1–22)

When Jesus used the example of Sodom and Gomorrah, he was emphatically speaking not about homosexuality but about hospitality. Jesus saw his disciples as being in a sense like those angels in the story of Sodom; indeed the Luke story specifies that Jesus was sending out teams in twos. (*He sent them on ahead of him in pairs... Luke 10:1*) Just as the two angels were bringing God's word to Sodom, so the disciples were to bring God's word to each town. But Jesus anticipated that they would not always receive a nice welcome. In the Matthew account, Jesus goes on to talk about the disciples being seriously abused.

Today, when people think of hospitality, they tend to think of someone throwing a pleasant party for friends or relatives. But in the Bible hospitality is all about *welcoming the stranger*. As the book of Hebrews put it, "Do not neglect to show hospitality to strangers, for by doing so some have entertained angels unawares." (Hebrews 13:2) The moral depravity of Sodom and Gomorrah—the self-centeredness and utter lack of caring—was expressed in the fact that the people did not welcome strangers to the town but treated them with severe abuse. The same moral depravity is repeated today whenever people mistreat those who are perceived as outsiders.

What then is the message of this story with regard to contemporary discussions about how the church should relate to LGBTQ people? The story is a clarion call to show gracious welcome to those outside one's own circle.

Chapter 2

So misunderstood is the story of Sodom that the English word "sodomy" was invented to denote homosexual practice. In reality, the story is all about the fundamental sin that affects every human being—the hardness of the human heart that results in the uncaring, abusive treatment of others. If there is anything that the story would move the church today to do, it is to embrace a spirit of compassion and show God's welcome—to all.

A Parallel to the Story of Sodom

In those days, when there was no king in Israel, a certain Levite, residing in the remote parts of the hill country of Ephraim, took to himself a concubine from Bethlehem in Judah. But his concubine became angry with him, and she went away from him to her father's house at Bethlehem in Judah, and was there some four months. Then her husband set out after her, to speak tenderly to her and bring her back. He had with him his servant and a couple of donkeys. When he reached her father's house, the girl's father saw him and came with joy to meet him. His father-in-law, the girl's father, made him stay, and he remained with him three days; so they ate and drank, and he stayed there. On the fourth day they got up early in the morning, and he prepared to go; but the girl's father said to his son-in-law, "Fortify yourself with a bit of food, and after that you may go." So the two men sat and ate and drank together; and the girl's father said to the man, "Why not spend the night and enjoy yourself?" When the man got up to go, his father-in-law kept urging him until he spent the night there again. On the fifth day he got up early in the morning to leave; and the girl's father said, "Fortify yourself." So they lingered until the day declined, and the two of them ate and drank. When the man with his concubine and his servant got up to leave, his father-in-law, the girl's father, said to him, "Look, the day has worn on until it is almost evening. Spend the night. See, the day has drawn to a close. Spend the night here and enjoy yourself. Tomorrow you can get up early in the morning for your journey, and go home."

But the man would not spend the night; he got up and departed, and arrived opposite Jebus (that is, Jerusalem). He had with him a couple of saddled donkeys, and his concubine was with him. When they were near Jebus, the day was far spent, and the servant said to his master, "Come now, let us turn aside to this city of the Jebusites, and spend the night in it." But his master said to him, "We will not turn aside into a city of foreigners, who do not belong to the people of Israel; but we will continue on to Gibeah." Then he said to his servant, "Come, let us try to reach one of these places, and spend the night at Gibeah or at Ramah." So they passed on and went their way; and the sun went down on them near Gibeah, which belongs to Benjamin. They turned aside there, to go in and spend the night at Gibeah. He went in and sat down in the open square of the city, but no one took them in to spend the night.

Then at evening there was an old man coming from his work in the field. The man was from the hill country of Ephraim, and he was residing in Gibeah. (The people of the place were Benjaminites.) When the old man looked up and saw the wayfarer in the open square of the city, he said, "Where are you going and where do you come from?" He answered him, "We are passing from Bethlehem in Judah to the remote parts of the hill country of Ephraim, from which I come. I went to Bethlehem in Judah; and I am going to my home. Nobody has offered to take me in. We your servants have straw and fodder for our donkeys, with bread and wine for me and the woman and the young man along with us. We need nothing more." The old man said, "Peace be to you. I will care for all your wants; only do not spend the night in the square." So he brought him into his house, and fed the donkeys; they washed their feet, and ate and drank.

While they were enjoying themselves, the men of the city, a perverse lot, surrounded the house, and started pounding on the door. They said to the old man, the master of the house, "Bring out the man who came into your house, so that we may have intercourse with him." And the man, the master of the house, went out to them and said to them, "No, my brothers, do not act so wickedly. Since this man is my guest, do not do this vile thing. Here are my virgin daughter and his concubine; let me bring them out now. Ravish them and do whatever you want to them; but against this man do not do such a vile thing." But the men would not listen to him. So the man seized his concubine, and put her out to them. They wantonly raped her, and abused her all through the night until the morning. And as the dawn began to break, they let her go. As morning appeared, the woman came and fell down at the door of the man's house where her master was, until it was light.

In the morning her master got up, opened the doors of the house, and when he went out to go on his way, there was his concubine lying at the door of the house, with her hands on the threshold. "Get up," he said to her, "we are going." But there was no answer. Then he put her on the donkey; and the man set out for his home. When he had entered his house, he took a knife, and grasping his concubine he cut her into twelve pieces, limb by limb, and sent her throughout all the territory of Israel. Then he commanded the men whom he sent, saying, "Thus shall you say to all the Israelites, 'Has such a thing ever happened since the day that the Israelites came up from the land of Egypt until this day? Consider it, take counsel, and speak out.'"

Judges 19

Chapter 3

Nearly a millennium after the story of Sodom and Gomorrah, a story unfolds in the hill country of the Promised Land, during the time of the Judges. It starts out as a simple story of a man and his concubine, and it ends in horrific brutality.

A concubine in Old Testament times was a woman in a kind of slave wife status, which did not mean that she had no rights or freedom but that she was obtained through purchase and was in a lesser status than a full "wife" would be. Concubines were common in the social landscape of the Late Bronze Age in the ancient near east. The first part of the story, in Judges 19, describes a woman who is a concubine, who leaves her husband after some sort of marital argument. The husband goes after her to try to win her back, which results in him spending several days with his father-in-law, who seems to want to keep visiting forever. Finally, late one day, the man departs with his concubine to head home, and they arrive just after sunset in the town of Gibeah, where they enter the town square, hoping to find a place to spend the night. This sets up a scenario that will parallel the story of Sodom and Gomorrah.

The Bible reports, "No one took them in to spend the night." (Judges 19:15) They did not, at least initially, find hospitality, even though Gibeah was an Israelite town, where one would think they would certainly be welcomed. But then the story continues, "In the evening there was an old man coming in from his work in the field… He said to them, 'Peace be to you. I will care for all your wants; only do not spend the night in the square.'" (Judges 19:16) This man, like Lot in city of Sodom, welcomes and cares for these strangers. He does so with magnanimity; as the story says, "So he brought them into his house, fed their donkeys, and they washed their feet and ate and drank." (Judges 19:20–21)

But the parallel with Sodom continues. The Scripture reports, "While they were enjoying themselves, the men of the city, a perverse lot, surrounded the house and started pounding on the door. They said to the old man, 'Bring out the man who came into your house, so that we may know him.'" (Judges 19:22) History repeats itself. As in the story of Sodom, there is a homosexual element in the story, but it is incidental; the moral issue is the perverse desire of the townspeople to rape the town's guests! In the end, the concubine is put out to the mob, and the men rape her all night until she is dead.

The husband in this story is certainly no saint—he abandons his concubine to the mob!—although it could be said that in putting out his own concubine, he was acting to save his host's daughter from a similar fate. In any case, the outrage of Israel will finally be directed against the gang of rapists. In grief, the husband cuts the body of his concubine into pieces and sends them to the twelve tribes of Israel as a grisly sign of the horrible crime that has taken place in Gibeah. The tribes in response raise an army, come against Gibeah, and burn the place to the ground. As the Scripture reports, "The whole city went up in smoke." (Judges 20:40) Gibeah thus receives the same judgment for sin as Sodom and Gomorrah did—going up in flames.

The outrageous sin that is described in each story is the same—the sin of violent abuse directed toward visitors. The stories in Genesis 19 and Judges 19–20 are set in very different time periods—nearly a thousand years apart—and have very different characters; yet the themes in the stories are remarkably similar. Both are stories involving attempted homosexual rape. In both stories, the sin of the crowd is not *homosexuality* but *violent abuse of the stranger*; and the moral value that is centrally commended is that of *hospitality*.

There is nothing in these stories that would move Christians to condemn LGBTQ persons. To the contrary, the condemnation falls upon those who would maltreat "outsiders." In both the Judges and Genesis stories, the righteous are those who receive others with grace.

Homosexuality in Biblical Times

The Old Testament Context

From the laws of Deuteronomy: *None of the daughters of Israel shall be a temple prostitute; none of the sons of Israel shall be a temple prostitute. You shall not bring the fee of a prostitute or the wages of a male prostitute into the house of the Lord your God in payment for any vow, for both of these are abhorrent to the Lord your God.*

Deuteronomy 23:17–18

From the time of King Rehoboam of Judah, late 10th century BC: *Judah did what was evil in the sight of the Lord; they provoked him to jealousy with their sins that they committed, more than all that their ancestors had done. For they also built for themselves high places, pillars, and sacred poles on every high hill and under every green tree. There were even male temple prostitutes in the land. They committed all the abominations of the nations that the Lord drove out before the people of Israel.*

I Kings 14:22–24

From the time of King Asa of Judah, early 9th century BC: *Asa did what was right in the sight of the Lord, as his ancestor David had done. He put away the male temple prostitutes out of the land, and removed all the idols that his ancestors had made.*

I Kings 15:11–12

From the time of King Jehoshaphat of Judah, mid-9th century BC: *Now the rest of the acts of Jehoshaphat, and his power that he showed, and how he waged war, are they not written in the Book of the Annals of the Kings of Judah? The remnant of the male temple prostitutes who were still in the land in the days of his father Asa, he exterminated.*

I Kings 22:45–46

From the time of King Josiah of Judah, late 7th century BC: *Then the king directed that all the elders of Judah and Jerusalem should be gathered to him. The king went up to the house of the Lord, and with him went all the people of Judah, all the inhabitants of Jerusalem, the priests, the prophets, and all the people, both small and great; he read in their hearing all the words of the book of the covenant that had been found in the house of the Lord. The king stood by the pillar and made a covenant before the Lord, to follow the Lord, keeping his commandments, his decrees, and his statutes, with all his heart and all his soul, to perform the words of this covenant that were written in this book. All the people joined in the covenant. The king commanded the high priest Hilkiah, the priests of the second order, and the guardians of the threshold, to bring out of the temple of the Lord all the vessels made for Baal, for Asherah, and for all the host of heaven; he burned them outside Jerusalem in the fields of the Kidron, and carried their ashes to Bethel. He deposed the idolatrous priests whom the kings of Judah had ordained to make offerings in the high places at the cities of Judah and around Jerusalem; those also who made offerings to Baal, to the sun, the moon, the constellations, and all the host of the heavens. He brought out the image of Asherah from the house of the Lord, outside Jerusalem, to the Wadi Kidron, burned it at the Wadi Kidron, beat it to dust and threw the dust of it upon the graves of the common people. He broke down the houses of the male temple prostitutes that were in the house of the Lord, where the women did weaving for Asherah.*

I Kings 23:1–7

From the book of Job: *The godless in heart cherish anger; they do not cry for help in bondage. They die in their youth, and end their life among the temple prostitutes.*

Job 36:13–14

Chapter 4

There are two verses in the book of Leviticus, considered in the next chapter, that condemn "a man lying with another male as with a woman." (Leviticus 18:22; 20:13) Modern readers see that wording and immediately think of gay men in a sexual relationship. But what would have come to the mind of an ancient Israelite who read those words? This is a critical question to ask, because it is only when we understand what the words meant to the original audience that we can rightly understand what the Scripture is saying to us. To answer the question, we need to look at the original context, as it is described in the historical books of the Old Testament.

When the people of Israel, after the deliverance from Egypt, settled in the land of Canaan, they found themselves living in close proximity to many Canaanite populations. This situation is spelled out in some detail at the beginning of the book of Judges. The Canaanites practiced an ancient polytheistic religion which shared some common ground with Biblical faith—as it was rooted in a basic awareness of a Divine Reality behind all things—but which differed sharply from Biblical faith in many of its specific ideas and practices. The Bible proclaims one God, whose chief characteristic is steadfast love (Hebrew: *hesed*), and who establishes a faithful covenant with human beings. Religious practices outlined in the Bible are a response to this sovereign Lord, who is clearly the prime Actor in the universe. Canaanite religion, on the other hand, envisioned the Divine as a pantheon of multiple gods, who were very much like enlarged human beings—imperfect and squabbling. As in many pagan religions, the gods were believed to be not particularly interested in human well-being. Canaanite religious practices, therefore, involved a set of rituals designed to spur the gods into favorable action.

For farming communities in the semi-arid land of Canaan, the chief concern was *fertility*—not just fertility in human childbearing, but the fertility of the land, to produce the food upon which people were directly dependent. Because of that concern, the most important god for people in the Canaanite pantheon was Baal—who was believed to be in charge of the weather. Canaanite worship came to be focused upon Baal, and also upon Asherah, also called Astarte, Baal's female consort. Baal was often depicted adorned with the horns of a bull or riding on the back of a bull—the bull being a symbol of fertility. Asherah was often depicted naked.

How does one spur a fertility god into action? There are numerous ancient references to *sacred prostitution* as a means of trying to do this in pagan religions. The worshipper's coitus with temple prostitutes would (in theory) arouse the gods, who would then bless one's land with fertility. This kind of fertility cult, utilizing at times both male and female temple prostitutes, appears to have existed in multiple places in the ancient near east. In recent decades there has been considerable debate among scholars over just how widespread such fertility cults were; scholars generally agree that they were by no means universal in the ancient world. But there is good evidence that sacred prostitution was utilized in particular cultures stretching from the lands of modern-day Turkey to modern-day Iraq, and there is strong evidence within the Bible itself that cult prostitutes were a key feature of Canaanite religion.

In the book of Deuteronomy, there is an ancient Israelite law that states,

"None of the daughters of Israel shall be a temple prostitute (*qedeshah*); none of the sons of Israel shall be a temple prostitute (*qadesh*). (Deuteronomy 23:17)

You shall not bring the fee of a prostitute (*zanah*) or the wages of a male prostitute (*kelev*) into the house of the Lord your God in payment for any vow, for both of these are abhorrent to the Lord your God." (Deuteronomy 23:18, NRSV)

This passage uses a structure that is very common in Biblical Hebrew called *parallelism*—in which two successive

Chapter 4

statements express very closely related ideas. The beginning phrase of each verse speaks of a *qedeshah* in the first verse and a *zanah* in the second. The Hebrew word *zanah* זָנָה is the general term in the Bible for an ordinary female prostitute. The word *qedeshah* קְדֵשָׁה, in a parallel position in the first line, also means "prostitute"; but it has another important aspect to its meaning, as the term is based on the word *qadosh* קָדוֹשׁ, which means "holy." To be "holy" in the Old Testament means to be set apart for religious service or devotion. So a qedeshah is a prostitute in service of a religious cult. The term in typically translated in English versions of the Bible as "shrine prostitute" (New International Version), "sacred prostitute" (New English Translation), or "temple prostitute" (New Revised Standard Version; New Century Bible). The term "temple prostitute" does not imply that these prostitutes were working in the tabernacle or in the temple in Jerusalem, but rather than they were associated with temples of Baal, or simple shrines to Baal, which were widespread.

The interplay between these two words for female prostitute comes out in a very early story in the Bible in Genesis 38, in the story of Tamar, who seeks to entrap her father-in-law, Judah, who was acting unjustly, by posing as a prostitute. The story says that "When Judah saw her, he thought she was a *zanah* (*common prostitute*)" (Genesis 38:15). He goes to buy her services, then leaves his staff with her as a guarantee that he will pay her later. When he subsequently sends his servant to pay the bill and retrieve his staff, the servant asks the men of the area, "Where is the *qedeshah* (*shrine prostitute*) who was sitting by the road?" (Genesis 38:21) Obviously, only a prostitute would be "sitting by the road," and of course Tamar was dressed as a prostitute. But the servant apparently attempts to dignify his master at this point, by suggesting that his master had not gone in to just an ordinary prostitute but had engaged in a religious act! Tamar, however, had long since change clothes and disappeared. The men reply, "There has not been any *qedeshah* (*shrine prostitute*) here." (Genesis 38:21b)

In addition to illustrating how *zanah* and *qedeshah* both refer to a prostitute, the Genesis 38 story shows how many in ancient Israel were loose in morals and in religious purity! The problem of Israelites being lured into the pagan religious practices of their neighbors would be a major issue, continuing for centuries.

In the law in Deuteronomy 23, the second half of each line refers to male prostitutes. Verse 17 says, "None of the sons of Israel shall be a *qadesh*." The word *qadesh* קָדֵשׁ is the masculine form of the word *qedeshah*; it thus means the same thing—temple prostitute—but with reference to males. This plainly refers to the fact that there were also male temple prostitutes in Canaanite religion. Since it was male worshippers who were engaging in the rituals to bring fertility to the land, this necessarily implies that there were homosexual acts involved.

The parallel phrase in verse 18 is "you shall not bring the wages of a kelev into the house of the Lord your God is payment for any vow." The Hebrew term *kelev* כֶּלֶב literally means "dog," but it appears here to be a slang term referring to a male prostitute—obviously a pejorative term! Notice that in verse 18—*You shall not bring the fee of a prostitute or the wages of a male prostitute into the house of the Lord your God in payment for any vow*—the concern is not with prostitution *per se* but with any involvement of prostitution with temple worship. The verse prohibits anyone from using money raised through prostitution to pay a temple obligation.

Verse 18 thus stands in close parallel with the concern of verse 17 that no one in Israel should work as a temple prostitute. The overarching concern of both verses is *to avoid mixing prostitution with worship*. The existence of this law in Deuteronomy is a clear indication that such an intertwining of prostitution and religion was a feature of Canaanite religion and an ever-present temptation for the people of Israel.

In spite of the fact that the people of Israel were to worship God alone and follow God's Law, the history of Israel shows that they were continually drawn into Canaanite religious practices. Often they would try to worship God and Baal simultaneously. A prime example of that is the story of Elijah, who criticized the people for wanting to follow both Baal and the Lord, and he finally challenged the prophets of Baal to a contest on the top of Mount Carmel (I Kings 18). The mixed religious devotion of the ancient Israelites has been confirmed archaeologically, as archaeologists have found pagan household idols in Israelite homes. Since Israelite farmers, like the Canaanites, were longing for a good harvest, it is easy to understand how they could be influenced by rituals that promised fertility.

The historical books of the Bible report an ongoing situation in which the Israelites were engaging in pagan worship, including cultic prostitution. The passages from I and II Kings cited at the beginning of this chapter show how difficult it was for even faithful kings to root out such pagan worship practices from the land. I Kings 14 reports that "the people of Judah built for themselves high places, pillars, and sacred poles on every high hill and under every green tree." (I Kings 14:23) The terms "high places," "pillars," and "sacred poles" refer to holy sites created for pagan worship. Notably, the passage specifically says "There were even male temple prostitutes in the land." (I Kings 14:24) The Hebrew word here is *qadesh*. This shows that *male temple prostitutes* were seen as uniquely characteristic of pagan worship.

The next chapter in I Kings reports that King Asa, a faithful king, took action to eliminate pagan rituals from the land of Judah. The Scripture reports, "He put away the male temple prostitutes out of the land and removed all the idols that his ancestors had made." (I Kings 15:11-12) Again, male temple prostitutes are specifically mentioned as an egregious problem. Nevertheless, Asa's efforts proved only partly successful, since his successor, Jehoshaphat, continued the project. In I Kings 22, there is once more a specific mention of male temple prostitutes, and Jehoshaphat's draconian efforts to get rid of them; as the Scripture reports, "The remnant of the male temple prostitutes who were still in the land in the days of his father Asa, Jehoshaphat exterminated." Repeatedly in I Kings, *male temple prostitutes* appear as a distinctively outrageous blemish upon Israel and as a threat to genuine faith.

In spite of such actions, pagan worship practices proved resilient. The same problems appeared two centuries later. II Kings reports how King Josiah acted to rid Judah of all the pagan elements that had infiltrated the land, even to the extent of pagan items and practices in the temple itself. As the Scripture says, "The king commanded the high priest Hilkiah, the priests of the second order, and the guardians of the threshold, to bring out of the temple of the Lord all the vessels made for Baal, for Asherah, and for all the host of heaven; he burned them outside Jerusalem in the fields of the Kidron, and carried their ashes to Bethel. He deposed the idolatrous priests whom the kings of Judah had ordained to make offerings in the high places at the cities of Judah and around Jerusalem; those also who made offerings to Baal, to the sun, the moon, the constellations, and all the host of the heavens. He brought out the image of Asherah from the house of the Lord, outside Jerusalem, to the Wadi Kidron, burned it at the Wadi Kidron, beat it to dust and threw the dust of it upon the graves of the common people. He broke down the houses of the male temple prostitutes that were in the house of the Lord, where the women did weaving for Asherah."

These passages reveal two central features of the cultural setting in ancient Israel: (1) there was an ongoing problem with the people of Israel being drawn into pagan worship

Chapter 4

practices, and (2) the existence of male temple prostitutes was seen as emblematic of the problem. What, therefore, would have come to mind for ancient Israelites when they heard a law forbidding "a man to lie with a another male as with a woman"? They would have immediately thought about the practice of male temple prostitutes.

They might also have thought about the two other occasions when homosexual behavior is mentioned in the Biblical story—in the attempted rape of men in Sodom and in Gibeah. Those two cases were related to a larger social feature of the ancient near east: homosexual rape was employed by men in various places to subjugate others and express dominance (as when armies conquered a people). The idea of "a man lying with a male" could call to mind this kind of brutality.

This exhausts the mention of homosexual activity in the historical materials of the Old Testament. Only two types of behavior are mentioned—prostitution and rape. There is no mention of lesbian behavior at all. There is thus nothing mentioned in the Old Testament that is remotely comparable to what people are talking about today when they think of same-sex adults in a loving, committed relationship.

One other feature of the Old Testament context deserves mention. For the ancient Israelites—a small people who remembered the command in Genesis to "be fruitful and multiply" and who also remembered that Abraham's descendants were supposed to become as numerous as the stars—the central purpose of sexual activity was understood to be procreation. In ancient thinking, the man's semen was thought to be the key element in creating a child—the woman was thought to be a vessel in which the child formed—so there naturally appeared to be something quite wrong for a man to expend his semen in a way that did not contribute to some sort of fertility. In the story of Onan, Onan "spilled his seed on the ground" (Genesis 38:9) instead of fulfilling his duty of enabling his deceased brother's wife to have a child. He was condemned. Onan's sin was primarily that of refusing to fulfill a sacred obligation to his family; but the story also illustrates the high importance of "using one's seed" to create new generations. In that context, the very idea of homosexual activity would appear inconsistent with the general command to "be fruitful."

In the Old Testament setting, everything related to homosexuality—the fertility cult, the rape of the guest, the problem of childlessness—was negative. The laws in Leviticus were shaped for this context. Only by keeping the historical setting in mind can we rightly understand these laws.

Selective Literalism and the Laws of Leviticus

You shall not lie with a male as with a woman; it is an abomination.
Leviticus 18:22

If a man lies with a male as with a woman, both of them have committed an abomination; they shall be put to death; their blood is upon them.
Leviticus 20:13

You shall keep my statutes. You shall not let your animals breed with a different kind; you shall not sow your field with two kinds of seed; nor shall you put on a garment made of two different materials.
Leviticus 19:19

When you build a new house, you shall make a parapet for your roof; otherwise you might have bloodguilt on your house, if anyone should fall from it.
Deuteronomy 22:8

A woman shall not wear a man's clothing, neither shall a man wear a women's clothing. Any who do so are an abomination to the Lord your God.
Deuteronomy 22:5

You shall not eat any detestable thing.
Deuteronomy 14:3

From among all the land animals, these are the creatures that you may eat. Any animal that has divided hoofs and is cleft-footed and chews the cud—such you may eat. But among those that chew the cud or have divided hoofs, you shall not eat the following: the camel, for even though it chews the cud, it does not have divided hoofs; it is unclean for you. The rock badger, for even though it chews the cud, it does not have divided hoofs; it is unclean for you. The hare, for even though it chews the cud, it does not have divided hoofs; it is unclean for you. The pig, for even though it has divided hoofs and is cleft-footed, it does not chew the cud; it is unclean for you. Of their flesh you shall not eat, and their carcasses you shall not touch; they are unclean for you.

These you may eat, of all that are in the waters. Everything in the waters that has fins and scales, whether in the seas or in the streams—such you may eat. But anything in the seas or the streams that does not have fins and scales, of the swarming creatures in the waters and among all the other living creatures that are in the waters—they are detestable to you and detestable they shall remain. Of their flesh you shall not eat, and their carcasses you shall regard as detestable. Everything in the waters that does not have fins and scales is detestable to you.

These you shall regard as detestable among the birds. They shall not be eaten; they are an abomination: the eagle, the vulture, the osprey, the buzzard, the kite of any kind; every raven of any kind; the ostrich, the nighthawk, the sea gull, the hawk of any kind; the little owl, the cormorant, the great owl, the water hen, the desert owl, the carrion vulture, the stork, the heron of any kind, the hoopoe, and the bat.

All winged insects that walk upon all fours are detestable to you. But among the winged insects that

walk on all fours you may eat those that have jointed legs above their feet, with which to leap on the ground. Of them you may eat: the locust according to its kind, the bald locust according to its kind, the cricket according to its kind, and the grasshopper according to its kind. But all other winged insects that have four feet are detestable to you.
Leviticus 11:2–23

Chapter 5

Many Christians have grown up hearing that you should read the Bible with the attitude that "it means what it says." In other words, you should understand the Bible in a simple, literal way. That approach is relatively novel in the history of Christianity. For most of church history, up until the last few centuries, Christian leaders were convinced that you are not supposed to read everything in the Bible in a literal way, because there are many sections in the Bible that are intended to be understood figuratively. It is also quite clear, as noted in the chapter above, that there are many passages that can only be rightly understood in light of their context. To read everything in the Bible in a simplistic, literal fashion would be to seriously distort God's Word.

In the book of Leviticus, there are two laws that refer to homosexual behavior. Notably, they only talk about male behavior. These are obviously not comprehensive statements about all kinds of same-sex relationships. But both verses are strongly negative about "a man lying with a male as with a woman." The second of the two verses concludes with a prescribed punishment, which is not only plain but emphatic—the phrase "their blood is upon them" means that their execution is entirely their own fault, and they shall receive no clemency.

Leviticus 20:13 seems very clear and straightforward. If it "means what it says," then anyone caught in a homosexual act should be executed. There have been times when Christians have established laws to this effect. In England, the last execution for homosexual behavior was in 1835, when two men caught in the act were hanged. Today there are still countries in which the practice of homosexuality is punishable by death, although they are all Muslim-majority countries following a certain understanding of *sharia*.

Today, most Christians who oppose the practice of homosexuality would want to drop the death penalty part of Leviticus 20:13. But this results in a logical contradiction. How do you decide that the first half of the verse "means what it says" but the second half does not? People who want to read the Bible literally thus become *selective literalists.* This pattern of selective literalism continues well beyond Leviticus 20:13.

There is a law in Deuteronomy that declares, "When you build a new house, you shall make a parapet for your roof; otherwise you might have bloodguilt on your house, if anyone should fall from it." (Deuteronomy 22:8) Do you have a fence around your roof? If not, you are breaking this Biblical law! There is a law in Leviticus that says, "You shall not sow your field with two kinds of seed." (Leviticus 19:19) Do you have more than one kind of plant in your garden? If so, you are going against what God's law plainly says! In the same verse there is a law that declares, "You shall not put on a garment made of two different materials." (Leviticus 19:19) The clothes you have on right now are probably against God's law, since their fabric is likely some sort of blend!

Such verses press us to recognize that context is critical. It makes no sense to take Biblical verses at face value and simply plop them into the present day. These verses do not "mean what they say," for in fact a literal understanding of these verses would result in a wrong understanding. To rightly understand the meaning, one must understand the concern that these verses are addressing in their original context, and then look for the relevant concern in the present-day setting. Only then can one consider how the principle embodied in the verse may be rightly applied to modern-day situations.

The law in Deuteronomy 22:8 was written when houses had flat roofs. People would use their roof as a patio. The Deuteronomy law required a fence, so as to prevent people from falling to injury or death. The relevant concern today is to keep people's safety in mind when building a structure. Deuteronomy 22:8 is important, not because of what it literally says about roof parapets, but because it is the conceptual Biblical foundation of all modern-day building codes! Clearly, the meaning of the verse is not the literal sense of it but a much deeper message—that we must think of the well-being of others when undertaking a project.

How then are we to understand the Leviticus verses about homosexuality? Why is it that whatever was being described in these verses was considered so serious that it called for the death penalty? The laws can only be rightly understood in light of their original context.

These verses are found in a section of Leviticus called the Holiness Code, in chapters 17 through 26. This was a long set of rules, many of them expressed in single verses, whose primary concern was to set the people of Israel apart from their pagan neighbors. Many earlier chapters in Leviticus have the same function—to make the people of Israel *distinctive*. The central issue being addressed by these verses was the ongoing tendency of the people of Israel to be drawn into paganism. As noted in the previous chapter, the Israelites repeatedly fell into the practices and beliefs of the peoples around them. God's call for the people of Israel was to chart a new spiritual course for humanity—to worship one God, and to approach God as One to be honored, trusted, and obeyed—in contrast to the pagan approach, which sought to manipulate a supposed pantheon of gods. But it was very easy for the Israelites to be influenced by their neighbors and to be pulled into the devotional practices of the surrounding culture. Modern Christians know this sort of problem. It is easy for Christians today to be drawn into the rampant materialism, the spiritual laxity, and the self-centered lifestyles that are so prominent in contemporary culture.

The problem of being overwhelmed by the surrounding culture was particularly acute for the early Israelites, as they were a tiny group of people in a sea of paganism. How could they possibly hold to a distinctive morality and spirualty in that setting? The answer provided by God in the book of Leviticus was a set of laws designed to create a wall of *separation* between the Israelites and their neighbors.

This was the purpose of the food laws in Leviticus. Leviticus says that you cannot eat pork, and you cannot eat shellfish, and you cannot eat insects (with the exception of crickets, grasshoppers, and locusts). Contrary to what people often suppose, these laws were not established out of health concerns. Human beings by this time had been eating pork for millennia and knew how to cook it. If there had been a problem with pork, other cultures would have restricted its use. But in fact all the pagan peoples in the area ate pork regularly, and the ones along the coast also ate shellfish. This is precisely why the people of Israel were told *not* to eat pork or shellfish—because if they did not eat pork or shellfish, they would not be sitting down at dinner tables with pagan people, getting influenced by pagan ideas! The food laws set the people apart, which was critical for a small people struggling to be faithful to God in the midst of a thoroughly pagan world.

The concern for *staying separate*, and not getting mixed into the surrounding culture, was what was behind the Leviticus laws about not mixing things. The people were not to mix different seed in one garden, or mix different fabrics in one garment, in order to enact, in their daily practices, the basic principle of staying separate.

There was a particular Hebrew word used to describe any action that could pull a person away from the right worship of God—the word *toevah* תּוֹעֵבָה. Something that was *toevah* was not necessarily something that was inherently evil; rather it was something which, if not avoided, would lead people to lose their spiritual moorings. In Deuteronomy 14, the term is used to denote the list of prohibited foods. Verse 3 says, "You shall not eat any *toevah*," and there follows a listing of those foods that you cannot eat, including pork and shellfish and insects. Obviously, eating such food is not intrinsically evil; but the foods were prohibited for the Israelites in order to help them to stay separate from pagan influence. The term *toevah* is likewise used in Deuteronomy 22, where it is used to denote "cross-dressing." Verse 5 says, "A woman shall not wear a man's clothing, neither shall a man wear a women's clothing. Any who do so are *toevah* to the Lord your God." It is hard to argue that there is something evil about wearing clothing normally worn by the opposite sex, especially since clothing styles change radically through time! But this was forbidden for the ancient Israelites as another way of practicing the separation principle of not mixing things. In short, the term *toevah* denotes something that was not always intrinsically wretched or wrong, but which the Israelites were to avoid as a way of steering clear of paganism.

This term is critical for our understanding of the Leviticus verses about homosexuality; because *toevah* is the key term in the two laws about the practice of homosexuality. Leviticus 18:22 says, "You shall not lie with a male as with a woman; it is *toevah*. Leviticus 20:13 says, "If a man lies with a male as with a woman, both of them have committed *toevah*.

How should one translate this term into English? This has been highly problematic for translators, because *toevah* is technical term that has no good English equivalent. Traditionally it has been translated into English as "detestable thing," "abhorrent thing," or "abomination"—translations which are misleading at best. With such a translation, the Deuteronomy verse about food, verse 14:3, reads, "You shall not eat any *detestable thing* (*toevah*)." (NIV, or "abhorrent thing" NRSV) With that translation, the verse suggests that shrimp or ribs must be considered detestable and abhorrent! Deuteronomy 22:5 has most traditionally been translated as, "All that do so [put on the clothing of the opposite sex] are an abomination (*toevah*) unto the Lord." (KJV) Since this was the translation read by American Christians for centuries, you can understand the longstanding conviction that women should not wear pants! Leviticus 18:22 and 20:13

have likewise been rendered, "You shall not lie with a male as with a woman; it is an *abomination* (*toevah*)" and "If a man lies with a male as with a woman, both of them have committed an *abomination* (*toevah*)." (King James Version, Douay-Rheims Version, New Revised Standard Version; the New International and Common English versions use the terms "detestable" or "disgusting.")

When American Christians assume that the Bible "means what it says," they are generally reading an English translation in their favorite version. When they read the word "abomination" in Leviticus 18:22 and 20:13, they quite naturally conclude that the Bible is declaring homosexual practice to be something dreadful, vile, and wretched. But this is not what the Bible is saying at all. The problem is that people have assumed a literal understanding of what is actually an inaccurate and misleading translation.

The word *toevah* appears more than one hundred times in the Old Testament. Its most common use is as a cultic term—describing some sort of pagan religious practice, which the Israelites were to avoid in order to steer clear of paganism. The term thus makes perfect sense in Leviticus 18:22 and 20:13, where the description of "a man lying with a male as with a woman" would connote the pagan practice of male temple prostitution. With this understanding, it is clear that the Leviticus verses are not a blanket condemnation of "the practice of homosexuality." They were specifically designed to keep the people of Israel separate from the practices of paganism.

This explains why the death penalty was prescribed in Leviticus 20. Because the danger of being swallowed up by pagan religions was so great for the ancient Israelites, the punishments for engaging in pagan practices were often severe. A prime example is the action of Elijah following the contest on Mount Carmel—he slew all the prophets of Baal. Such punishments seem horribly excessive today; but in the ancient context—when the faith of Israel was a fragile enterprise that could easily collapse—strident action to protect against paganism appeared necessary. Leviticus prescribed death for "a man lying with a male" precisely because the practice of male temple prostitution was seen as a mortal threat to Israelite faith, requiring severe countermeasures—which is exactly what one sees in the books of Kings.

From all this it is plain that these Leviticus verses are not talking about loving committed relationships between LGBTQ persons such as people think about today. The concern of these verses is with circumstances that were completely different from the present-day context. Moreover, it is notable that the great bulk of the Holiness Code in Leviticus is now believed by Christians to no longer apply to the present time. The reason for this—and the implications for the verses about homosexual practice—will be the subject of the next chapter.

Why Would Laws in Leviticus No Longer Apply?

About noon the next day, as they were on their journey and approaching the city, Peter went up on the roof to pray. He became hungry and wanted something to eat; and while it was being prepared, he fell into a trance. He saw the heaven opened and something like a large sheet coming down, being lowered to the ground by its four corners. In it were all kinds of four-footed creatures and reptiles and birds of the air. Then he heard a voice saying, "Get up, Peter; kill and eat." But Peter said, "By no means, Lord; for I have never eaten anything that is profane or unclean." The voice said to him again, a second time, "What God has made clean, you must not call profane." This happened three times, and the thing was suddenly taken up to heaven.

Now while Peter was greatly puzzled about what to make of the vision that he had seen, suddenly the men sent by Cornelius appeared. They were asking for Simon's house and were standing by the gate. They called out to ask whether Simon, who was called Peter, was staying there. While Peter was still thinking about the vision, the Spirit said to him, "Look, three men are searching for you. Now get up, go down, and go with them without hesitation; for I have sent them." So Peter went down to the men and said, "I am the one you are looking for; what is the reason for your coming?" They answered, "Cornelius, a centurion, an upright and God-fearing man, who is well spoken of by the whole Jewish nation, was directed by a holy angel to send for you to come to his house and to hear what you have to say." So Peter invited them in and gave them lodging.

The next day he got up and went with them, and some of the believers from Joppa accompanied him. The following day they came to Caesarea. Cornelius was expecting them and had called together his relatives and close friends. On Peter's arrival Cornelius met him, and falling at his feet, worshiped him. But Peter made him get up, saying, "Stand up; I am only a mortal." And as he talked with him, he went in and found that many had assembled; and he said to them, "You yourselves know that it is unlawful for a Jew to associate with or to visit a Gentile; but God has shown me that I should not call anyone profane or unclean. So when I was sent for, I came without objection. Now may I ask why you sent for me?"

Cornelius replied, "Four days ago at this very hour, at three o'clock, I was praying in my house when suddenly a man in dazzling clothes stood before me. He said, 'Cornelius, your prayer has been heard and your alms have been remembered before God. Send therefore to Joppa and ask for Simon, who is called Peter; he is staying in the home of Simon, a tanner, by the sea.' Therefore I sent for you immediately, and you have been kind enough to come. So now all of us are here in the presence of God to listen to all that the Lord has commanded you to say."

Then Peter began to speak to them: "I truly understand that God shows no partiality, but in every nation anyone who fears him and does what is right is acceptable to him. You know the message he sent to the people of Israel, preaching peace by Jesus Christ—he is Lord of all. That message spread throughout Judea, beginning in Galilee after the baptism that John an-

nounced: how God anointed Jesus of Nazareth with the Holy Spirit and with power; how he went about doing good and healing all who were oppressed by the devil, for God was with him. We are witnesses to all that he did both in Judea and in Jerusalem. They put him to death by hanging him on a tree; but God raised him on the third day and allowed him to appear, not to all the people but to us who were chosen by God as witnesses, and who ate and drank with him after he rose from the dead. He commanded us to preach to the people and to testify that he is the one ordained by God as judge of the living and the dead. All the prophets testify about him that everyone who believes in him receives forgiveness of sins through his name."

Acts 10:9–43

Chapter 6

For Christians today, all the Old Testament laws which were designed to keep the people of Israel separate and to avoid mixing with their neighbors have been *dropped*—completely dropped from the practice of the church. We mix all sorts of fabrics together. We plant all sorts of different seeds in the same garden. We eat pork and lobster and shrimp and crab (for which many Christians are thankful!) Why did the church drop all of the laws having to do with keeping separate from the world?

It is because, according to the book of Acts, God told the leaders of the church that those laws no longer apply; and the reason for that is because the followers of Jesus Christ are no longer to keep separate from the world but are to go out into the world to all people with the gospel. This was the message that came clearly to Peter in the story in Acts 10, when he was told in a vision that the food laws are no longer applicable and that Christians can eat anything. He realized, he said, that "God shows no partiality" (Acts 10:34). He was not to separate himself from certain others but was to reach out to everyone with the good news of Jesus Christ. Following the vision, he went to the home of Cornelius, a Roman centurion, and shared the gospel. Today Christians continue to follow the message of Peter's vision. The separation laws of Leviticus no longer apply; Christians are not to withdraw from the world but are to reach out to it.

If those two verses in Leviticus about male sexual activity had to do with keeping the Israelites distinct from pagan religion, and if all the laws in Leviticus that aimed to keep the people separate from pagan culture have now been dropped, it follows that those two verses also no longer apply. Indeed we do not have a problem with male temple prostitutes today. Consider this: if the law against eating pork did not mean there is something inherently wrong with eating pork, and if the law against mixing fabrics did not mean there is something inherently wrong with your cotton/polyester blend, then the law in Leviticus against homosexual activity did not mean that there is something inherently wrong with all same-sex relations. These laws were from a particular historical context, in which people were trying to resist the pagan influences of their day. What Christians rightfully carry forward into the present day are not the specific prohibitions but the spiritual principle—that we need to resist the cultural influences that would draw us away from God in our own time. That would mean resisting materialism, disbelief, hedonism, racism, promiscuity, and other such cultural patterns that are a threat to genuine faith today. At the same time, we are not to condemn or separate ourselves from any other *people*. When Peter reached out to Cornelius, he was reaching out in love to a Gentile and a Roman military officer who would have been despised by most Jews of the day. His outreach provided a clear message to Christians of all ages that we are to despise no one. Christians are to reach with the grace of Christ to all.

Homosexuality in Biblical Times

The New Testament Context

When he entered Capernaum, a centurion came to him, appealing to him and saying, "Lord, my servant is lying at home paralyzed, in terrible distress." And Jesus said to him, "I will come and cure him."

Matthew 8:5–7

Chapter 7

When it comes to same-sex practices, there is a significant shift from the ancient near eastern context of the Old Testament to the Greco-Roman context of the New Testament. Although there is a possibility that temple prostitution—including same-sex rituals—was practiced in some places (this is much debated among scholars), and although armies were still in the practice of humiliating their conquered foes, the major new element in Greco-Roman culture was the popularity of the man-boy relationship. There was a widespread practice of adult men having sexual relations with boys who had not yet passed through puberty. Some of these boys were willing participants; many others were sex slaves, called catamites. The practice was thoroughly condemned in Jewish circles, and it received some critique in Greco-Roman circles as well, but it was common in many places. This provides the context for several New Testament references to homosexuality.

This is the backdrop for the one place in the gospels whee there might be an oblique reference to homosexuality. The gospel of Matthew relates an incident in which a centurion came to Jesus, saying, "Lord, my servant is lying at home paralyzed, in terrible distress." (Matthew 8:5, NRSV, NIV). The Greek word translated here as "servant" is not the normal word for servant, which would be *doulos*. The word rather is *pais* παῖς, which indicates a youth. The centurion was asking help for his servant boy. While there is no direct indication in the story that there was something sexual between the centurion and his *pais*, it is quite certain what some people in the crowd would have been thinking. The people around Jesus were mostly Jewish; the story took place in Capernaum, a Jewish town on the north shore of the Sea of Galilee. They would not have thought much of the centurion in the first place, since a Roman army officer was considered an instrument of the hated occupation; and they would have been well aware that centurions, along with others who had money and power in the Greco-Roman world, sometimes had a servant boy—a *pais*—who did more than just the housework. When the centurion said, "My boy is lying at home..." there were surely some eyebrows raised.

What is notable is how Jesus responded in this setting. Jesus said, "I will come and cure him." (Matthew 8:6) There was no hesitation and not the least bit of concern about what people might have been thinking. What was an issue for some in the crowd was no issue for Jesus. He was concerned purely about healing, and he treated the centurion and the servant boy as persons of worth. Jesus thus provides a very clear model for how we should treat all people—as human beings worthy of God's love.

In addition to the man-boy activity, there were other kinds of same-sex relationships, among both men and women, that were prevalent in the Greco-Roman world. There were multiple standard Greek terms used to denote persons involved in those relationships; but those terms do not find their way into the New Testament. Instead, what receives steady reference in the New Testament is the general climate of sexual morality (or lack thereof) in Greco-Roman society. The world of the Roman Empire was characterized by sexual looseness, promiscuity, and excess, and it is such behavior that the New Testament repeatedly condemns. The word *porneia* (πορνεία), meaning fornication, appears in some form (either as a noun or verb) 44 times in the New Testament. The word *epithumia* (ἐπιθυμία), meaning lust, appears 56 times. The word *aselgeia* (ἀσέλγεια), indicating sexual wantonness and translated licentiousness or lasciviousness, appears 9 times in the New Testament. The raucous state of sexual morality in the Greco-Roman world was epitomized by the Emperor Caligula, who was on the throne when the apostle Paul started his ministry. Caligula committed adultery multiple times, had numerous catamites and other young lovers, forced himself sexually on many people, and committed incest with his sisters. He was the very picture of sexual perversion and excess.

Chapter 7

In one of the few New Testament references to same-sex activity, in Romans 1, Paul would use the phrase "degrading passions" to refer to same-sex behavior. (Romans 1:26) These words fit within a much larger context in the letter to the Romans, which will be discussed in a following chapter; but it is easy to see what Paul would have had in mind when he wrote those words. Within the Greco-Roman setting, he was surely referring to the sort of sexual wantonness and boundless lust that were exemplified by Caligula and widespread in Roman society. The continual accent in Paul's writings is on the general problem of promiscuity and the call for Christians, in contrast, to live in sexual purity. When he speaks, therefore, in a condemning way of "degrading passions," he certainly is not thinking of a committed lifelong loving relationship between two LGBTQ persons such as people might think about today! Paul's overarching critique, throughout his letters, is against the sexual looseness that was rampant on every level of the larger society.

In sum, there is little specific reference to same-sex relationships in the New Testament; the scant references that exist will be discussed in the following chapters. The broad accent is on the call to sexual fidelity—a call that is surely pertinent in our own time, and relevant to everyone.

The Homosexual Behavior Condemned by Paul

Live by the Spirit, I say, and do not gratify the desires of the flesh. For what the flesh desires is opposed to the Spirit, and what the Spirit desires is opposed to the flesh; for these are opposed to each other, to prevent you from doing what you want. But if you are led by the Spirit, you are not subject to the law. Now the works of the flesh are obvious: fornication, impurity, licentiousness, idolatry, sorcery, enmities, strife, jealousy, anger, quarrels, dissensions, factions, envy, drunkenness, carousing, and things like these. I am warning you, as I warned you before: those who do such things will not inherit the kingdom of God.

Galatians 5:16–21

Do you not know that wrongdoers will not inherit the kingdom of God? Do not be deceived! Fornicators, idolaters, adulterers, male prostitutes, sodomites, thieves, the greedy, drunkards, revilers, robbers—none of these will inherit the kingdom of God. And this is what some of you used to be. But you were washed, you were sanctified, you were justified in the name of the Lord Jesus Christ and in the Spirit of our God.

I Corinthians 6:9–11

Now we know that the law is good, if one uses it legitimately. This means understanding that the law is laid down not for the innocent but for the lawless and disobedient, for the godless and sinful, for the unholy and profane, for those who kill their father or mother, for murderers, fornicators, sodomites, slave traders, liars, perjurers, and whatever else is contrary to the sound teaching that conforms to the glorious gospel of the blessed God, which he entrusted to me.

Timothy 1:8–11

Chapter 8

The letters of Paul often speak of the moral impact of the gospel. The fact that Jesus displayed mercy toward all, including people in various circumstances who were guilty of serious sin, did not mean that sinful behaviors were to be overlooked or approved. When forgiving the woman caught in adultery, for example, Jesus said, "Go and sin no more." (John 8:11) The gospel message is one of spiritual transformation. As people turn from sin in repentance and experience the mercy of Christ, they are freed from sin and empowered to live a good life. Paul would thus distinguish between "life in the Spirit"—the morally good life that people can follow when they are filled with the Spirit of Christ—and "life in the flesh," which is life still in bondage to sin. (see Romans 8).

This emphasis on the moral impact of the gospel led Paul to draw sharp distinctions between good patterns of living versus bad patterns. On that theme, he often used a literary technique that was quite common in Greek discourse, whereby he would provide *lists* of contrasting good and bad behaviors. One such list is in Galatians chapter 5.

Paul writes, "Live by the Spirit, and do not gratify the desires of the flesh." (Galatians 5:16) By desires of the flesh, he does not simply mean bodily desires. People desire food all the time, and there is nothing wrong with that (unless you are working on a diet!). The phrase "desires of the flesh" is a common phrase Paul uses to denote sinful desires, as opposed to spiritually healthy desires. He then elaborates on what he is talking about by moving into a list of prime sinful behaviors.

He writes, "The works of the flesh are obvious: fornication, impurity, licentiousness, idolatry, sorcery, enmities, strife, jealousy, anger, quarrels, dissensions, factions, envy, drunkenness, carousing, and things like these." (Galatians 5:19–21) There are fifteen items in this list, besides the final extension of "things like these." Two items in the list relate to sexual behavior—*fornication* (πορνεία *porneia*) and *licentiousness* (ἀσέλγεια *aselgeia*)—terms referring to general sexual wantonness and promiscuity. The terms apply to everyone and are certainly relevant to today's culture! There is no mention of same-sex relations in the list.

This naturally raises the question: If same-sex relations were considered to be a sin, a moral problem requiring disapproval by the early church, why is there no reference in this list, especially when the list includes fifteen items, two of them relating to sexual practices? This is one of many examples in the Bible of a place where human sinfulness is being extensively discussed, and same-sex relationships are simply not mentioned—which raises the question as to whether there ought to be an issue here in the first place. Perhaps same-sex relationships were not a problem in the particular community (or communities) to which Paul writing in Galatia, a possibility to which we will return.

Another list of sinful behaviors appears in I Corinthians chapter six, in which there *is* reference to same-sex behavior—making this one of the most oft-cited passages in the present debate. Paul begins by saying, "Do you not know that wrongdoers will not inherit the kingdom of God?" (I Corinthians 6:9); and he then continues with another list: "fornicators, idolators, adulterers, male prostitutes, sodomites, thieves, the greedy, drunkards, revilers, robbers" (I Corinthians 6:9-10). Two words are of key significance—*malakoi* μαλακοὶ, translated in the NRSV as "male prostitutes," and *arsenokoitai* ἀρσενοκοῖται, translated in the NRSV as "sodomites."

The previous discussion of the Leviticus passages noted the problems with English translations of the technical Hebrew term *toevah*; and similar problems arise with these terms in I Corinthians. Neither *malakoi* nor *arsenokoitai* is the normal Greek term for gay or lesbian persons. The terms become quite understandable, however, when we keep in mind the widespread practice of pederasty in the Roman world.

Chapter 8

In Greco-Roman society, the boys who were typically used in man-boy sexual relationships were boys who had not yet gone through puberty. Once a boy began to develop body hair, coarser skin, and adult male traits, he was no longer considered to be sexually desirable; and furthermore, since he was becoming a man, it was considered unmanly of him to be on the receiving end of sexual penetration. In ancient Greco-Roman writings, one can find multiple examples of adult men ruing the day when their "boy" began to lose his soft, smooth skin and started to become an adult.

The word *malakos* in I Corinthians 6 is a common Greek word that means "soft." In its usage in verse 9 (*malakoi*) it is in the plural and literally means "softies." In the Greco-Roman context it is obvious what this means—it is a slang term referring to those boys.

The word *arsenokoitai* is more obscure. It is a *hapax legomenon*—a word appearing uniquely in its context. Within existing Greek documents from the period, there is no other appearance of the term, making it difficult to translate! Some suggest that Paul himself coined the word from the Septuagint, the Greek translation of the Old Testament, from Leviticus 20:13, where the word *arsenos* (*man*) appears with the word *koiten* (*to go to bed with*) in the prohibition against "a man lying with a man." On this basis, it is sometimes argued that *arsenokoites* (the singular form of the word) would simply mean "man-bedder" or "homosexual." But if Paul wanted to refer to homosexual behavior generally, there was no need for him to invent a word, since there was already a range of clear terms in the Greek language for him to use! Moreover, if he in fact invented the word straight out of Leviticus, its meaning would more rightly be understood as "male temple prostitute." (There are some who argue that the term should be understood in this way.)

But in fact it is highly questionable that Paul would use a verse from the Greek translation of *Leviticus* in order to invent a word that he would introduce in writing to *Corinth*.

Many in the Corinthian congregation were of Gentile background—the letters to Corinth reflect issues facing people who were accustomed to Gentile ways of living—and so the Corinthian church, where people were not so familiar with the Hebrew Scriptures, would have been the least likely place to use a brand new invented word based upon an obscure Old Testament verse! It is more likely that Paul was using a term understood by his audience, which has simply not been found in the limited Greek documents that we have from the period.

A likely possibility suggested by some scholars is that the term had been invented earlier by Jewish rabbis, who drew the term out of the language of Leviticus but used it specifically as a pejorative term to denote the man-boy sexual practices that they observed—and despised—among the Gentiles. In that case, Paul would have been using a current term that would have been ideally suited to what he was talking about in I Corinthians.

What is clear from the form of *arsenokoites* is that it must be referring to some sort of homosexual behavior; but it must be a specific kind of activity, since there were more general terms available to refer to gay and lesbian relationships. The form of the word indicates that it refers to the active partner in some sort of homosexual relationship. The meaning of the word becomes very plain when we note that it is juxtaposed to the word *malakoi*. Since Paul has just referred to the boys who were the passive partners in the man-boy relationship, it makes sense that he then immediately refers to the active partners—the men who made use of those boys.

Arsenokoitoi is thus best translated as pederasts, and in fact this is how it has historically been translated into multiple languages. When Martin Luther did his translation of the Bible into German in the sixteenth century, he translated *arsenokoitai* as *Knabenschänder*—a German word that specifically means men who abuse boys, or pederasts. The same terminology is used in modern German translations. A corresponding word appears in Dutch translations (*knapenschenders*) and also in French translations (*les pédérastes*) of I Corinthians 6.

With this understanding of *arsenokoitai* and *malakoi*, it makes perfect sense that these terms appear in the list of sinful behaviors in the letter to the Corinthians and not in the corresponding list in the letter to the Galatians. The recipients of the letter to the Galatians were Jewish Christians who were inclined to hold firmly to the Jewish law; they would not have been engaging in Greco-Roman style man-boy relationships. Corinth, on the other hand, was a Greek port city full of traders and sailors, a place especially known for its debauchery. It is highly likely that boys were being used there as prostitutes, as well as in the longer term man-boy relationships popular in the Greek world. This was an obvious, ever-present issue for the Christians in Corinth, and thus a specification of the problem in the "list of sinful behaviors" in the first letter to the Corinthians was most appropriate.

But if *arsenokoitoi* means "pederasts," how is it that it got translated into English as "sodomites"? It goes back to the King James Bible, when in 1611 the translators in England working under King James rendered the term in I Corinthians 6 as "them that defile themselves with mankind." *Malakoi* was rendered as "effeminate." Ever since then, English translations have rendered these terms very broadly. The New International Version translates both terms together as "men who have sex with men." The Common English Bible translates the terms as "both participants in same-sex intercourse." The term "sodomites," used in the New Revised Standard Version, is itself an outdated term based on a false understanding of the story of Sodom and Gomorrah, and of course it also is a broad term meant to refer to all gay sexual activity.

Once again, as American Christians read their English Bibles, they are reading words which they assume to be the Biblical Word, but which in fact are a serious deviation from what the Bible actually says. I Corinthians 6 is not talking about same-sex relationships in general. What is condemned as immoral in I Corinthians 6 is what we would all very well condemn—the practice of pederasty, which continues to be a serious problem today. It has been a devastating problem in the Catholic Church, and it affects our whole society.

The same problem of pederasty is addressed in the list of sinful behaviors in I Timothy, where once again the word *arsenokoitai* is employed. The passage reads, in the New Revised Standard Version, 'The law [of God] is laid down not for the innocent but for the lawless and disobedient, for the godless and sinful, for the unholy and profane, for those who kill their father or mother, for murderers, fornicators, sodomites (*arsenokoitai*), slave traders, liars, perjurers, and whatever else is contrary to the sound teaching that conforms to the glorious gospel of the blessed God." (I Timothy 1:9–11) The word *malakoi* does not appear, perhaps because it was not the boys themselves who were to be condemned, but rather the whole abusive practice and the adults responsible. But once again the term arsenokoitai has been very inaccurately translated into English. In the NRSV it is translated as "sodomites" and in the New International Version as "those practicing homosexuality." The Common English Bible translation is even further off the mark, as it renders the term "people who have intercourse with the same sex," which would include lesbians, even though the term in Greek encompasses only men.

All this highlights the major challenge for Christians today who wish to rightly understand what the Bible says about human sexuality, but who are using versions of the Bible that contain historically biased and misleading translations of the original Greek or Hebrew. Only by carefully studying the original languages and the original context will we be able to "rightly explain the word of truth." To think that I Corinthians 6 and I Timothy 1 are calling Christians to condemn LGBTQ persons is to completely miss the point. The central moral issue highlighted by Paul is the issue of child abuse—an issue of great and ongoing relevance for our own time.

Is Same-Sex Activity Unnatural and to Be Judged?

For the wrath of God is revealed from heaven against all ungodliness and wickedness of those who by their wickedness suppress the truth. For what can be known about God is plain to them, because God has shown it to them. Ever since the creation of the world his eternal power and divine nature, invisible though they are, have been understood and seen through the things he has made. So they are without excuse; for though they knew God, they did not honor him as God or give thanks to him, but they became futile in their thinking, and their senseless minds were darkened. Claiming to be wise, they became fools; and they exchanged the glory of the immortal God for images resembling a mortal human being or birds or four-footed animals or reptiles.

Therefore God gave them up in the lusts of their hearts to impurity, to the degrading of their bodies among themselves, because they exchanged the truth about God for a lie and worshiped and served the creature rather than the Creator, who is blessed forever! Amen.

For this reason God gave them up to degrading passions. Their women exchanged natural intercourse for unnatural, and in the same way also the men, giving up natural intercourse with women, were consumed with passion for one another. Men committed shameless acts with men and received in their own persons the due penalty for their error. And since they did not see fit to acknowledge God, God gave them up to a debased mind and to things that should not be done. They were filled with every kind of wickedness, evil, covetousness, malice. Full of envy, murder, strife, deceit, craftiness, they are gossips, slanderers, God-haters, insolent, haughty, boastful, inventors of evil, rebellious toward parents, foolish, faithless, heartless, ruthless. They know God's decree, that those who practice such things deserve to die—yet they not only do them but even applaud others who practice them.

Romans 1:18–32

Chapter 9

When reviewing the references in the Bible to same-sex activity, it quickly becomes apparent that what few references there are deal with very specific circumstances that involve aberrant behavior. The Old Testament contains two cases of attempted homosexual rape, and it condemns male temple prostitutes. The New Testament condemns pederasty. In what we have considered so far, there has been no reference to same-sex activity generally, and there has been no reference to women in same-gender relationships at all.

The sole exception to this in the Bible is in the letter to the Romans. The first chapter of Romans contains the one passage in the Bible that mentions lesbian as well as gay activity, and it is the one passage that speaks of same-sex relationships in a broad, generalized fashion. For this reason, this is the Biblical passage people most often quote with reference to same-sex activity. The passage appears to be clearly and strongly negative toward same-sex activity. But before we assume we know how to take this, it is crucial to consider the larger context of these verses; because in the letters of Paul there are a number of statements which seem to be saying one thing, but which actually mean something quite different—when the total context of Paul's writings is kept in view.

For example, in another place, in the first letter to Timothy, Paul says, "Let a woman learn in silence with full submission. I permit no woman to teach or to have authority over a man; she is to keep silent." (I Timothy 2:11–12) That seems quite clear, and it is on the basis of this that a number of churches, such as Catholic, Orthodox, and conservative Protestant churches, do not allow woman pastors, and restrict women's roles in the church generally. If you take this verse at face value, it appears that Paul believed that women should be excluded from leadership in the church.

But in fact, Paul did not believe that, which is quite plain from the larger context of Paul's ministry. In one of his most important early churches, the church in Corinth, Paul installed a woman as the lead pastor, Priscilla, who provided strong leadership along with her husband, Aquila. She clearly taught and had spiritual authority over men in the church. In view of this dissonance between Paul's actions in Corinth and the words in I Timothy, some scholars argue that the letter to Timothy could not have been written by Paul but must have been written by a later person in his name. (There are a number of reasons for this argument.) But it is possible to uphold Pauline authorship for I Timothy and to understand why he might have said those words about women in leadership, by keeping in mind that this was an instruction for a particular cultural setting.

Timothy was serving in Ephesus, where the primary pagan religion revolved around the cult of the goddess Artemis, whose great temple was in Ephesus. Paul knew firsthand the powerful influence of the cult of Artemis; Artemis worshippers had at one point rioted against his preaching. In the cult of Artemis, women played a prominent role, and it appears that at the time of Timothy there were women in the Ephesian church who were promoting beliefs and practices drawn from the cult of Artemis. Their leadership presented a real threat to the Ephesian congregation, where many people still had in mind the ideas and patterns of Artemis religion. This explains why Paul would tell Timothy to command these women to be silent, even when there were women preachers elsewhere! From the larger context of Paul's ministry, it is plain that this rule against women preachers should not be taken as a rule for everywhere and for all time. It only makes sense as a part of Paul's general principle that the presentation of the gospel needs to be adapted to each cultural setting. In the Ephesian context, the backdrop of the cult of Artemis made women's leadership in that church problematic. Today, when the cultural context is not a history of idol-worshipping priestesses but a history of male-dominated priesthoods, the church should *want* women in leadership, in order to make the most effective witness to our own time.

Chapter 9

The issue of context is very important in another place, where Paul says, "Slaves, obey your earthly masters with fear and trembling, in singleness of heart, as you obey Christ; not only while being watched, and in order to please them, but as slaves of Christ, doing the will of God from the heart." (Ephesians 6:5–6) This verse seems to accept the institution of slavery and urges slaves to simply and obediently fulfill their assigned role. In centuries past, some churches used this verse to justify the practice of slavery. If you take this verse at face value, it appears that Paul thought that slavery is God-ordained and appropriate. But in fact Paul did not think that, which is quite clear when you look at his letter to Philemon, in which Paul, while accepting that slavery was a legal institution in the Roman Empire, urged Philemon to set a slave free on the basis of Christian values. Paul's admonition to slaves to submit to their masters was thus not a general affirmation of the practice of slavery; it was an encouragement to live in the most Christlike way possible no matter where one finds oneself.

In Romans one, there are two verses where Paul seems to say that when women engage in relations with women or men with men, it is contrary to nature and an expression of our fallen human condition. But once again it is crucially important to look at the larger context of those two verses.

When Paul wrote the letter to the Romans, he was in the late part of his life, and this letter would be his most comprehensive statement about salvation and the righteousness of God. He was writing to both Jews and non-Jews, or Gentiles, but this presented a challenge, because Jews felt that they were in a very different position with regard to salvation than Gentiles. In the typical Jewish understanding, Jews had the inside track with God, and Gentiles were hopeless sinners. Paul addressed this thinking at the outset. (Later in the letter, he would address the opposite problem—that Gentiles who had accepted Jesus considered themselves superior to Jews.)

In chapter one, Paul begins to describe the Gentile position from the traditional Jewish perspective. He writes, "What can be known about God is plain to them, because God has shown it to them. Ever since the creation of the world God's eternal power and divine nature, invisible though they are, have been understood and seen through the things God has made. So they are without excuse; for though they knew God, they did not honor him as God or give thanks to him, but they became futile in their thinking . . . Claiming to be wise, they became fools; and they exchanged the glory of the immortal God for images resembling a mortal human being or birds or four-footed animals or reptiles." (Romans 1:19–23)

Paul thus establishes that even though Gentiles did not have the history of Biblical revelation, they are still accountable to God. The reality of God is plain for them to see, since God's power and glory are evident everywhere, and everyone has a basic God-implanted sense of right and wrong. Gentiles therefore have "no excuse" when they turn from away from God and refuse to do what is right and engage in all sorts of idolatry.

This whole line of argument was not unique to Paul. It was standard rabbinical argumentation—the sort of thing Paul would have heard over and over when he stood with the conservative Jewish leadership and was named Saul. The argument that Paul lays out can be found, for example, in the Wisdom of Solomon, a Jewish tract from the second century BC, which is now a part of the collection we call the Apocrypha, which was never accepted by the Jews as Scripture, but which reflected Jewish thinking at the time. Paul's arguments in Romans 1 closely echo a number of specific points made in the Wisdom of Solomon. He also uses a good bit of vocabulary that is unusual for his letters. In other words, Paul is not exactly speaking here in his own voice; he is portraying standard ideas that Jewish people in his day had about Gentiles. Paul might affirm some of those ideas, but his argument will move in a very interesting way.

Chapter 9

The Jewish book, the Wisdom of Solomon, after noting that Gentiles had fallen into the foolishness of idolatry, then makes the point that this resulted in all kinds of immoral behavior. Paul follows this line of argument exactly, as he continues and says, "Therefore God gave the Gentiles up in the lusts of their hearts to impurity, to the degrading of their bodies among themselves. (Romans 1:24) To say that "God gave them up" is a way of saying that God allowed people the freedom to go ahead and made bad moral choices. In this verse, Paul uses very broad terms—"impurity," and "the degrading of their bodies"—to denote the full scope of the negative and damaging things that people do.

The Wisdom of Solomon then continues further by listing a number of specific sins that were seen to be widespread in the ancient world. Among those specified in the Wisdom of Solomon was one called "exchanging of nature" (γενέσεως ἐναλλαγή Wisdom of Solomon 14:26), which seems to be a general reference to lesbian or gay sexual activity. Paul continues with exactly this idea, when he says, "Their women exchanged natural intercourse for unnatural, and in the same way also the men, giving up natural intercourse with women, were consumed with passion for one another. Men committed shameless acts with men and received in their own persons the due penalty for their error." (Romans 1:26–27). This is clearly a reference not just to a specific homosexual practice such as pederasty but to the entire scope of gay and lesbian activity.

It is these two verses that form a primary basis for traditionalist views about sexuality. Same-sex relations are described here as "unnatural." People often point to this to argue that only heterosexuality is natural and that any same-sex relations are contrary to God's design. But that is not actually what Paul is saying. In verse 26, the Greek phrase that he uses which is translated as "unnatural" is the phrase *para physin* παρὰ φύσιν. This was an oft-used phrase in the Greco-Roman world, where its standard meaning was not so much "unnatural" but more "atypical" or "unconventional." It did not indicate something immoral, but it did often have a somewhat negative connotation. Something was *para physin* when it was something that struck you as "just not right."

That is exactly how Jewish people in the first century viewed the same-sex practices that were widespread in the Greco-Roman world. Jews saw those same-sex practices as emblematic of Gentile culture and how the Gentiles, in their view, were just not right; they were, in the Jewish view, morally off. But significantly, Paul chose this particular phrase, *para physin*, which does not actually indicate something that is sinful. This is quite plain as the letter of Romans progresses, because a little later, in chapter 11, verse 24, Paul says that God acts *para physin*. God does so, Paul says, when God acts to include the Gentiles in God's plan of salvation even though the Jews were the chosen people. That act of bringing the Gentiles into the Jewish tree of life was, Paul, said, like grafting a wild olive branch onto a cultivated olive tree. Such an act was "unnatural" (*para physin*) in the sense that it was unconventional and unexpected. But this creates an extraordinary kind of word play. The very phrase that is used to describe Gentile same-sex activity, which was so condemned by the Jews, is the exact phrase that is later used to describe *God* when God includes those Gentiles in God's plan of salvation. When you are reading Romans 1, you do not see this coming. It is part of Paul's careful crafting of Romans 1, which sets up a later—and surprising—turn.

Along with the reference to same-sex activity, the Wisdom of Solomon continues with a listing of numerous sinful behaviors that were considered to be characteristic of the Gentile world. Again, Paul follows the Wisdom of Solomon with a final section in which he says, "They were filled with every kind of wickedness, evil, covetousness, malice. Full of envy, murder, strife, deceit, craftiness, they are gossips, slanderers, God-haters, insolent, haughty, boastful, inventors of evil, rebellious toward parents, foolish, faithless, heartless, ruthless. They know God's decree, that those who practice such things deserve to die—yet they not only do them but even applaud others who practice them." (Romans 1:29–32)

This is a thoroughgoing indictment of the Gentile world. Notice how Paul repeatedly refers to what "they" do. "They" are filled with every kind of wickedness. "They" are gossips, slanderers, and so forth. The same pattern can be seen in this entire section. It begins, "They are without excuse, for though they knew God they did not honor God." (Romans 1:20–21) "They became futile in their thinking." (Romans 1:21b) "Therefore God gave them up to impurity." (Romans 1:24) "Their women exchanged natural intercourse for unnatural." (Romans 1:26) "And since they did not see fit to acknowledge God, God gave them up to a debased mind and to things that should not be done." (Romans 1:28) "They" appear quite obviously to be very bad people!

A word meaning "they" or "their" appears 26 times in this section. This is highly unusual for Paul. Paul typically addresses the reader directly. His letters talk about what *you* should believe and what *you* should do and how *you* should deal with your own sin. Paul never spends a lot of time talking about "them" and how bad "they" are. But Romans 1 has the character that it does because Paul in this entire section is echoing standard Jewish rhetoric toward Gentiles, such as is reflected in the Wisdom of Solomon. He is not so much speaking in his own voice as he is voicing the kinds of condemning statements that Jewish speakers would typically level toward Gentiles.

In doing so, Paul was utilizing an ancient Greco-Roman rhetorical technique called προσωποποιΐα *prosopopoeia*, which means "speaking in the voice of another." This was a common rhetorical tool. In literature it was used to portray a particular perspective. In debate, it could be used to state another person's argument—for the purpose of finally refuting it. Paul in Romans chapter 1 has lined out the whole standard Jewish argument for why the Gentiles are guilty, godless, and immoral, and thus uniquely deserving of condemnation. But if this is prosopopoeia, there will be a turn, a pivot, in which Paul will dramatically reverse course, adopt his own voice, and rebut that entire argument that was just laid out.

Reading through Romans 1, the average Jewish person at the time would have been cheering Paul on. "Yes, Paul," the person would have been thinking, "you are right about those rotten Gentiles. They are corrupt. They are debased. They are full of immorality. They deserve to be condemned!" Then Paul continues,

"You have no excuse, whoever you are, when you judge others; for in passing judgment on another you condemn yourself, because you, the judge, are doing the very same things." (Romans 2:1)

This is a dramatically abrupt turn, absolutely jarring to the reader. Modern readers tend to miss the full impact of this, because centuries ago, as the Scriptures were divided into chapters and verses to make the study of them easier for everyone, this verse was made the beginning of chapter two, which can lead the modern reader to imagine that a new subject is starting here. But the original Greek was seamless. There is that long diatribe against those sinful Gentiles, and then suddenly Paul reverses from talking about *them* to talking about *you*. And the "you" specifically addressed is anyone who has been caught up in passing judgment on others. Suddenly the person with "no excuse" is the person who judges others and who thereby condemns the self. Paul thus establishes a point that will be foundational for his letter to the Romans. He will state it clearly in Romans 3—"*All* have sinned and fall short of the glory of God." (Romans 3:23)

Those two verses in Romans 1 that speak in a negative way about same-sex practices are often called the "clobber verses" of Romans, because they are regularly used to clobber LGBTQ people with sense that they are being condemned by the Bible. But the actually clobbering occurs in Romans 2, where Paul comes down hard on anyone who would pass judgment on others. Those two negative verses about sexuality in Romans 1 are part of a section expressing a judging attitude, which Paul, in the end, *refutes*. Paul's basic point is that we all stand as sinners before God, a point that he continues to hammer home all the way through chapters two and three. Therefore we are to pass judgment on no one. It is a teaching that clearly echoes Jesus' words in the Sermon on the Mount when he said, "Judge not, that you be not judged." (Matthew 7:1)

What then is to be said about the statement that same-sex activity is "unnatural?" That statement is also part of the judging attitude that Paul rejects. It may be that same-sex activity is "unconventional" in a society's eyes, but that does not make it sinful. Indeed God often acts *"para physin"*—in unconventional ways! Human beings may often be inclined to look down on those who are "different," but the very shape of God's activity shows that to be "atypical" is not to be out of line with God.

The whole thrust of the letter to the Romans is to disabuse the reader of any claim to self-sufficient righteousness and any propensity to stand in judgment over others. Paul makes plain that we are all in the same spiritual place—equally in need of the saving grace of Jesus Christ.

The error so often made in reading Romans—as well as other letters of Paul—is that people will read a small section in isolation without paying attention to how it functions in relation to the whole book and the entire corpus of Pauline material. Romans chapter 1 can only be rightly understood in light of the whole argument of the letter. Paul's sustained message throughout Romans is that salvation comes to everyone as a gift of God's grace; therefore no one can claim to be righteous, except for the righteousness that is given through Jesus Christ.

Strange Flesh

Even as Sodom and Gomorrah, and the cities about them in like manner, giving themselves over to fornication, and going after strange flesh, are set forth for an example, suffering the vengeance of eternal fire.
                                    Jude 1:7, KJV

Chapter 10

The limited New Testament references to same-sex behavior come to a conclusion in the book of Jude, where there is a reference sometimes cited in the present debate, which however may not refer to same-sex behavior at all. Verse seven mentions that the people of Sodom and Gomorrah "gave themselves over to fornication." The Greek word here is *ekporneusasai* ἐκπορνεύσασαι, a form of that familiar word *porneia*; in this case it is a verb form meaning "to indulge in fornication." This does not necessarily mean same-sex fornication, although, in light of the story of Sodom and Gomorrah, Jude may very well have in mind the lustful desire of the men of Sodom to rape the town's visitors. The next phrase is quite precisely translated in the King James Version when it speaks of the men of Sodom "going after strange flesh." The word translated "strange" is the Greek word *heteras* ἑτέρας, which indicates something that is of another sort. Sometimes people want to argue that this is a reference to the men in Sodom desiring other men, but that would force an odd interpretation on the phrase, since the wording "another sort of flesh" would be understood as referring to people of the same sex. It is much more likely that the phrase "strange flesh" refers to the fact that in the story of Sodom the men were trying to rape *angels*. This would connect to a reference to angels in the previous verse.

The point of the verse in Jude is to provide an illustration of punishment coming upon the wicked. It does not tell us anything about Sodom that we did not already know—that the men of Sodom were a depraved lot, who sought to engage in sexual violence against strangers and who were so outlandish in their behavior that they actually ended up assaulting angels. This has virtually nothing to do with caring relationships between LGBTQ people today.

What God Creates Is Good

Then God said, "Let us make humankind [adam] in our image, according to our likeness; and let them have dominion over the fish of the sea, and over the birds of the air, and over the cattle, and over all the wild animals of the earth, and over every creeping thing that creeps upon the earth." So God created humankind [adam] in his image, in the image of God he created them; male and female he created them.
Genesis 1:26–27

God saw everything that he had made, and indeed, it was very good.
Genesis 1:31a

The Lord God took the man [adam] and put him in the garden of Eden to till it and keep it. And the Lord God commanded the man, "You may freely eat of every tree of the garden; but of the tree of the knowledge of good and evil you shall not eat, for in the day that you eat of it you shall die."

Then the Lord God said, "It is not good that the man should be alone; I will make him a helper as his partner." So out of the ground the Lord God formed every animal of the field and every bird of the air, and brought them to the man to see what he would call them; and whatever the man called every living creature, that was its name. The man gave names to all cattle, and to the birds of the air, and to every animal of the field; but for the man there was not found a helper as his partner. So the Lord God caused a deep sleep to fall upon the man, and he slept; then he took one of his ribs and closed up its place with flesh. And the rib that the Lord God had taken from the man he made into a woman and brought her to the man. Then the man said,

"This at last is bone of my bones and flesh of my flesh; this one shall be called Woman [ishah] for out of Man [ish] this one was taken."

Genesis 2:15–23

Chapter 11

In addition to the direct references in the Bible to same-sex behavior—which are few—there are other passages which have major implications for our understanding of human sexuality. One such passage is the story of the creation of humanity in the book of Genesis.

When people talk about God creating human beings, there is a long-standing quip that "God created Adam and Eve, not Adam and Steve." The suggestion is that God created people with certain defined male and female natures, and that any departure from that would be a departure from God's design. But is this actually the message of Genesis?

The book of Genesis does not in fact say that God created a man named Adam, since Adam in ancient Hebrew is not a name. In Hebrew, *adam* (pronounced *ah-dahm*) is a word that means "human being." Genesis 1:27 says that "God created *ha-adam* הָאָדָם—*the* (*ha*) *human being* (*adam*), or as the New Revised Standard Version puts it, "God created humankind." The word *adam* does not specify any gender or orientation, which is why after saying that God created "the *adam*," the passage goes on to say that God created people "male and female." When the story of creation is continued in chapter two, it says that "God put *ha-adam*—the human being—in the Garden of Eden." (Genesis 2:15) English translations are typically misleading at this point, as they commonly say that God put a "man" in the garden, and they go on to describe the man doing one thing or another, which leads people to imagine a male figure in the garden. But the actual Hebrew uses the word *adam* consistently at this point; the figure God puts in the garden is the *adam*, the human being—gender unspecified.

The garden is paradise. It is beautiful and bountiful. But God says, "It is not good that the *adam* should be alone; I will make a suitable helper." (Genesis 2:18) There follows the story of God creating all sorts of animals and bringing them to the *adam*, who names each one. But, the story reports. "for the *adam* there was not found a partner." (Genesis 2:20) So

God causes a deep sleep to fall upon the human being, and creates another person from the rib; and it is then that two new Hebrew words are introduced in the story of the garden—*ish*, meaning man, and *ishah*, meaning woman. As the Scripture reports, "This one shall be called *ishah* (woman), having been taken out of *ish* (man)." (Genesis 2:23)

One of the major challenges people have when thinking of the Genesis story is that they tend to have in mind a certain traditional way of envisioning the story, backed up by traditional paintings of the story. We picture a man and a woman in a garden. But the actual picture in Genesis is more complex—it is of an androgynous human being who is literally pulled into pieces to finally make a man and a woman. The actual picture says that our humanity is much deeper than the sexual aspects of us; and therefore the principles laid out in Genesis transcend sexuality.

Genesis lays out foundational truths about who we are as human beings. The central truth is that *we are created by God, and what God creates is good*. The phrase "and God saw that it was good" follows immediately upon every description of what God creates in the first two chapters of Genesis. This means that however people are made, whether they have black skin or white, whether they are tall or short, whether they are super high functioning or differently abled, they are a good creation of God.

What then can be said about sexual orientation? All the scientific research into sexual orientation and gender identity has shown that people experience their sexual orientation and gender identity as a given. One cannot choose to be something other than what one is. Efforts to take people through "conversion therapy" to try to change their sexual orientation have been disastrous failures. Sexual orientation and gender identity are now clearly established as being among the many traits that are a part of a person's nature. Since Genesis declares that it is God who creates people as they are, and that what God creates is good, then being

LGBTQ is by no means an aberration or a sinful condition. It is a particular way of being a part of the marvelous and diverse creation of God.

On this basis, one must affirm that everyone has the same starting point—every person is created in a way that is good and worthwhile in God's sight. Everyone will have moral decisions to make from that point—whether a person is morally good will be the result of those decisions—but no one is in some "worse state" that puts the person into a disadvantaged position at the outset. If God is good and just—as the Bible repeatedly affirms—the moral playing field must be the same for everyone.

What then are the moral expectations for human beings with regard to their sexuality? The clear overall message in the Bible is that sexuality is meant to be expressed within a loving, lifelong commitment, that is, within marriage. Adultery and promiscuity are condemned, while sexual expression within the marriage covenant is strongly affirmed. These principles are broadly upheld by Christians of all different persuasions as comprising the moral framework . . . for at least heterosexual persons. But are there are different moral expectations for LGBTQ persons?

When Christians condemn the "practice of homosexuality," they are saying that LGBTQ persons must never express their sexuality. Since they cannot change their sexual orientation, and since marriage (in the traditional view) is forbidden to them, they only have one moral option—to commit to lifelong celibacy. But if this is the case, then the moral playing field is absolutely not the same for everyone, as God has apparently created a certain group of people with a set of moral expectations that are completely different from what is expected of everyone else. But how can God's moral law be inconsistent? The idea that LGBTQ persons can never express their sexuality conflicts further with the basic Genesis concept that what God creates is good. If LGBTQ persons are a part of the good creation of God, how can their

God-given sexuality be so unworthy or so amiss that it can never be allowed expression? Genesis also affirms that "it is not good for a person to be alone" (Genesis 2:18) How then can it be that LGBTQ persons must commit to remaining alone lifelong? It is true that single people can find very meaningful fellowship in friendships and in extended family and in communities. Yet heterosexual singles always have the option of marriage. Why would God create some people with a certain sexual orientation with the intention that they would never be allowed to find a partner?

When churches claim that LGBTQ persons must adhere to lifelong celibacy, in order to be right with God, they are making an extraordinary claim which is extremely tenuous on Biblical grounds. It is a claim that does not stand up well against the teachings of Genesis. In the next chapter, we will examine how well that claim stands up to the teaching of Jesus.

Is Celibacy the Christian Rule for LGBTQ Persons?

Jesus said to them, "Not everyone can accept this teaching, but only those to whom it is given. For there are eunuchs who have been so from birth, and there are eunuchs who have been made eunuchs by others, and there are eunuchs who have made themselves eunuchs for the sake of the kingdom of heaven. Let anyone accept this who can."

Matthew 19:11–12

Chapter 12

Jesus never said anything about homosexuality; but he did have something to say about celibacy. He offered a succinct and clear teaching when he said: "Not everyone can accept this teaching, but only those to whom it is given. For there are eunuchs who have been so from birth, and there are eunuchs who have been made eunuchs by others, and there are eunuchs who have made themselves eunuchs for the sake of the kingdom of heaven. Let anyone accept this who can." (Matthew 19:11–12)

A eunuch was a man, typically serving in an ancient king's court, who was surgically altered so as to be unable to molest the women in the king's harem. This is the middle group to which Jesus refers—those who have been "made eunuchs by others." A later chapter will discuss an important story about such a eunuch in the book of Acts. There would also be some people who have a congenital, biological hindrance to sexual activity; they would be the "eunuchs who have been so from birth." Then there would be those, Jesus said, "who have made themselves eunuchs for the sake of the kingdom of heaven." This does not suggest that some people are performing surgery on themselves! This refers to people who choose lifelong celibacy as a part of serving God. In the present day, that of course would include Catholic priests.

There are thus three kinds of celibacy—biologically given, imposed by others, or chosen—and the whole thing is framed by Jesus with the statements, "Not everyone can accept this teaching" and "let anyone accept this who can." The clear message is that lifelong celibacy is not something that is to be expected of people. It is a given for some; it is chosen by others. But when Jesus said, "Not everyone can accept this," he was plainly saying that lifelong celibacy cannot be considered a moral requirement.

Based on overall Biblical teaching about sexuality, one would certainly say that celibacy is the right stance for certain periods of life. Most Christians encourage young people to abstain from sexual activity until marriage; because according to the Bible, sexual activity is intended for the covenant of marriage. Jesus' whole statement about eunuchs comes right after a discussion about marriage. Most counselors, including secular ones, would also urge people to abstain from sexual activity during bereavement, because people need to go through a process of grief and emotional healing.

Lifelong celibacy is something else. One might choose, of course, to live a celibate life. The apostle Paul said that if you are single and celibate, it is actually best to remain that way; because you save yourself a whole lot of trouble! Moreover, he noted, you can devote yourself more fully to God. On other hand, he said, if you must... if you are burning with passion... go ahead and get married! (see I Corinthians 7) For a single person, who is heterosexual, there is always a possibility of entering marriage. Lifelong celibacy is never a requirement.

But in the stance that has become the "traditional" stance of many churches, lifelong celibacy *is* the requirement for LGBTQ people. This stance conflicts directly with the plain teaching of Jesus. Since Jesus taught that lifelong celibacy can be chosen but is never to be imposed upon people, it is simply contrary to the truth of Jesus to insist that a certain group of people must commit to lifelong celibacy.

The moral logic of the Bible requires that the same moral principles, values, and laws should be applied to everyone. This means that sexual ethics must be the same for everyone. That sort of ethical coherence leads inevitably to the idea that the opportunity of marriage—and the moral values of faithfulness and commitment—should apply to LGBTQ persons just as much as to heterosexual persons. But can such a position be sustained on a Biblical foundation? This will be the subject of the next chapter.

Marriage in the Biblical Understanding

Therefore a man leaves his father and his mother and clings to his wife, and they become one flesh.
                                               Genesis 2:24

Some Pharisees came to him, and to test him they asked, "Is it lawful for a man to divorce his wife for any cause?" He answered, "Have you not read that the one who made them at the beginning 'made them male and female,' and said, 'For this reason a man shall leave his father and mother and be joined to his wife, and the two shall become one flesh'? So they are no longer two, but one flesh. Therefore what God has joined together, let no one separate." They said to him, "Why then did Moses command us to give a certificate of dismissal and to divorce her?" He said to them, "It was because you were so hard-hearted that Moses allowed you to divorce your wives, but from the beginning it was not so. And I say to you, whoever divorces his wife, except for unchastity, and marries another commits adultery."
                                            Matthew 19:3–9

Chapter 13

Biblical teaching about marriage begins with the story of the man and woman in the garden, with the observation, at the end of Genesis chapter 2, that "a man leaves his father and mother and clings to his wife, and they become one flesh." (Genesis 2:24). People today sometimes take this verse to mean that marriage is meant to be one man plus one woman. In Old Testament times, however, no one understood marriage this way. A common pattern in Old Testament days was that marriage was one man plus multiple women! Many of the most prominent Old Testament figures, such as Jacob or David, had numerous wives. It should be noted that polygamy in the Old Testament period served an important social function. In an era when there were more women than men—especially because of the constant warfare in that time—and when women could scarcely sustain themselves economically if they were single, polygamy provided the avenue for all women to become part of a marriage, wherein they would find not only a livelihood but also the possibility of childbearing, which in that society was the primary way for a woman to achieve fulfillment and status in the community. Polygamy was thus the approved model for marriage in Old Testament times—at least for men who could afford it!

The people who practiced polygamy would not have considered themselves to be deviating from the principle that in marriage "a man leaves his father and mother and clings to his wife, and they become one flesh." In polygamous marriage, people indeed left their parent's homes and became joined in a union that was deep and lifelong. The essence of marriage was that committed union.

Polygamy was an appropriate model for the circumstances of the ancient near east. But the fact that it was the accepted marriage model for thousands of years did not mean that it was God's intention for marriage for all time. The ideal model for marriage would change by the New Testament time period.

Cultural circumstances related to marriage had become quite different by the first century, when the numerical imbalance between the sexes was not nearly as great as in times past, and women had greater economic opportunities in the society. The New Testament, for example, mentions Lydia, who was a merchant (of purple cloth) with significant financial resources. With polygamy no longer needed to address social imbalances, monogamy became the rule, and this was the case throughout the Roman Empire by the time of Jesus (although there were exceptions). Within the Jewish community, there may still have been certain types of polygamy allowed—particularly in the case of "levirate marriage," when a man married his deceased brother's wife in order that she might bear children in the deceased brother's name. But monogamy was the general practice. It was in that context that divorce became a major issue.

It was a question about divorce that led to Jesus' most quoted statement about marriage. In general, Jesus said relatively little about marriage. He condemned adultery, and also warned against lust, in the Sermon on the Mount. He said that there is no marriage in heaven, when arguing with the Sadducees about the promise of resurrection. He is generally understood to have offered his blessing to marriage by attending a wedding feast at Cana of Galilee. And then he sharply critiqued divorce.

The gospel of Matthew reports that "Some Pharisees came to Jesus, and to test him they asked, 'Is it lawful for a man to divorce his wife for any cause?'" (Matthew 19:3) They were hoping to ensnare Jesus is a messy argument about proper grounds for divorce. But Jesus, as usual, surprised them with his answer.

He answered, "Have you not read that the one who made them at the beginning 'made them male and female,' and said, 'For this reason a man shall leave his father and mother and be joined to his wife, and the two shall become one flesh'? So they are no longer two, but

one flesh. Therefore what God has joined together, let no one separate." (Matthew 19:4–6)

When the argument in churches is made against same-sex marriage, this passage is the one most often cited, with the argument being that Jesus speaks here of "male and female" and describes marriage as "a man leaving his father and mother and being joined to his wife." But as is so often the case when reading the Bible, one must to do more than lift a few phrases out of the Bible in order to "rightly explain the word of truth." It is crucial to look at the whole structure of Jesus' argument here, along with the context of his words, in order to comprehend what he is in fact saying.

Jesus' statement is an answer to a question about divorce. The issue up front is not the sexes involved in marriage but the nature of the marriage covenant. In Jesus' day, it had become commonplace that men would divorce their wives for no good reason (except that their eye had fallen upon someone else, or they saw some other kind of personal advantage in a divorce). A classic contemporary case was that of Herod Antipas, who, while married to Phasaelis, fell into lust with his half-brother's wife Herodias. He divorced Phasaelis to marry Herodias (while she divorced her husband). The whole sleazy business was condemned by John the Baptist, which literally cost him his head.

In Roman society, divorce was easy to obtain and frequently practiced, especially by those in the more elite levels of society, who might see a particular remarriage as an opportunity for social advancement. In Jewish communities, divorce was also widespread. The Old Testament Law about divorce in Deuteronomy 24 had specified simply that, if a husband divorced his wife, he must give her a "certificate of divorce." In the original context, this was actually a social advance for women; the previous practice in the ancient near east had been that a husband simply had to verbally repudiate his wife in order to divorce her. The requirement that he must provide a certificate of divorce ensured that the woman would at least have a legal document to prove her marital status in the future. But by the first century, the Deuteronomy law had come to be seen as a justification for a broadly easygoing attitude toward divorce. As the Pharisees expressed it in their question, "Is it lawful for a man to divorce his wife for any cause?"

Notice that the question had to do with a man divorcing his wife. While it was legally possible under Roman law for a woman to divorce her husband, it was the rare Jewish woman who would divorce her husband, since for most Jewish women a divorce would be an economic disaster. Although women had more opportunity in the Roman period than in earlier times, it was still very difficult for women in lower socioeconomic classes to be suddenly out of the house and divorced. In a situation where "a man could divorce his wife for any cause," women were exposed to serious peril. The actual practice of divorce in the first century was causing a great deal of injustice against women.

What would Jesus say about this? The Pharisees were hoping to lure Jesus into a debate that was going on at the time among Jewish rabbis over the proper grounds for divorce. Although everyone agreed that divorce was permissible, there were sharp disagreements over the appropriate reasons for divorce, and the Pharisees saw plenty of opportunity to trip Jesus up here. But as he so often did when answering the Pharisees, Jesus quickly moved past their legalisms to get at the heart of the matter.

Jesus began by quoting Scripture. He said, "Have you not read that the one who made them at the beginning 'made them male and female,' and said, 'For this reason a man shall leave his father and mother and be joined to his wife, and the two shall become one flesh'?" (Matthew 19:4-5) The words quoted are from the creation story in Genesis 1:27 and 2:24. The simple quotation of the verses does not tell us much about what Jesus was thinking. These verses were often quoted by rabbis at the time in discussions about marriage, since they suggest that marriage has been a part of God's plan for humanity since the beginning. What is significant is not the quotation of the verses but the commentary that Jesus would make about them. What is the point that Jesus would make, based on these Scriptures, about marriage?

Jesus made his point using the classic Hebrew form of parallelism—giving the same basic message in two parallel statements, in order to emphatically drive his point home. The first statement he made after quoting Genesis was, "So they are no longer two, but one flesh." (Matthew 19:6a) Jesus thereby declared that a profound unity is created in marriage. His second statement, "Therefore what God has joined together, let no one separate" (Matthew 19:6b), emphasizes again the unity that God creates in marriage. The concluding phrase, "let no one separate," is a final rejection of the cavalier attitude toward divorce that prevailed in Jesus' day.

Jesus says nothing in these statements about the sexes involved in marriage. The entire message that he draws from the Genesis verses is about the inviolability of the marriage covenant. His point is consistent with what ancient Hebrews had perceived about marriage—that marriage in its essence is a committed union between persons. On that ground he rejected the easygoing divorce attitude of his day, which was bringing harm to many women.

When people want to make the passage in Matthew 19 talk about the sexuality of people in marriage, they are focusing on the verses that are quoted from Genesis rather than on what Jesus says about those verses. The point that Jesus makes, doubled in his parallel statements, is entirely this: Marriage, grounded in God's design for human beings, is intended to be an indivisible, lifelong union. It is a point that could be applied just as much to same-sex marriage as to heterosexual marriage! The words, "Therefore what God has joined together, let no one separate" could be spoken at any wedding.

If Christians wish to take Jesus' words in Matthew 19 in a simple, straightforward, and literal fashion, they must condemn all divorce ("except for unchastity," as Jesus says). Some Christians do take that position. It is interesting, however, that many conservative Christians today are inclined to make allowances for divorce . . . even as they reject same-sex marriage. The stance of Jesus in Matthew 19 is precisely the opposite. He says nothing about the sexes involved in marriage, while quite emphatically rejecting divorce. Jesus concludes his conversation with the Pharisees by saying, "Whoever divorces his wife, except for unchastity, and marries another commits adultery." (Matthew 19:9) Why is there so much focus today on trying to prevent a form of marriage, namely same-sex marriage, when the entire focus of Jesus was on trying to prevent divorce?

Does this mean that most divorce is to be condemned? Once again, to "rightly comprehend the word of truth," one must do more than lift a verse out of Scripture and try to make it say everything. It is crucial to understand the words of Jesus within both the specific context of the setting and the larger context of his overall teaching. In the specific context of the first century, Jesus was certainly condemning how women were being treated in his day. In the larger context of his teaching, Jesus' strong words against divorce must also be understood in light of his overall message about grace—that as human beings fall short of even our own best ideals, we have a God who forgives and restores and creates new beginnings. Jesus in Matthew 19 upholds the ideal that marriage is to be an unbreakable, lifelong union. Most couples entering marriage do so with a desire to embrace that ideal! But within our human frailties, marriages at times fall apart. There may be blame on one side or the other or both; but what is certain in virtually every divorce is that on both sides there is pain. What is the word of the gospel in such a time? In light of the whole teaching of Jesus, the gospel message clearly is that God meets people in the midst of their failures and pain with grace. Through Jesus Christ, there is forgiveness for all shortcomings, and there is the possibility to begin again. For this reason, churches have strong Biblical reason to support people going through divorce, and to celebrate the new beginnings that happen with remarriages.

The words of Jesus in Matthew 19 are all about the value and integrity of marriage. It would be against the spirit of Jesus to use these words to condemn people who sought to create a good marriage but whose marriage collapsed. It would be even more against the spirit of Jesus' teaching to use these words to try to keep people out of marriage altogether! Jesus in Matthew 19 is giving strong affirmation to marriage. He does not offer any comment about the sexes in marriage. He certainly is not seeking to exclude people from marriage. His teaching rather addresses the very heart of what marriage is—the commitment of two persons to a profound union, blessed by God, in which they are joined together, not in an easily disposable pairing, but in a covenant that, with God's help, will bring lifelong fulfillment.

Might not such a union be celebrated by same-sex couples? Some Christians today have great difficulty with the whole idea of same-sex marriage not so much because the Bible speaks about same-sex marriage (it does not) but because the church has never recognized same-sex marriage—over the course of 2,000 years. It seems a novel idea, conflicting with what marriage has "always been." Yet the Bible itself shows that there have been different models for marriage that have been considered appropriate for different time periods, according to the circumstances of the time. For 2,000 years after Abraham, polygamy was the approved model for God's people, until it was supplanted by monogamy alone around the time of Jesus. Today, humanity has come, for the first time, to understand sexual orientation and gender identity. This puts us at another watershed moment—when our understanding of marriage is being expanded to include same-sex couples.

Sometimes people fear that allowing same-sex marriage would threaten heterosexual monogamous marriage. But why would including more people in the covenant of marriage threaten the institution of marriage? If the essence of marriage is that it is a committed union, would it not be better to have more commitment? Indeed why would the church want to deny to a particular group of people a God-given blessing—marriage—that it strongly advocates for everyone else?

Same-sex marriage is not mentioned in the Bible simply because it was not in the cultural understanding of people at the time; but there is nothing in the Bible that would preclude same-sex marriage. To the contrary, the moral values that the Bible upholds for marriage—commitment, faithfulness, trust, cooperation, ability to forgive, authentic love—apply just as well to same-sex marriage as to heterosexual marriage. Including LGBTQ persons in marriage allows the sexual ethics of the Bible to finally be applied consistently—to all.

The Welcome of Jesus and the Dynamic of "Welcoming the Sinner, Not the Sin"

He entered Jericho and was passing through it. A man was there named Zacchaeus; he was a chief tax collector and was rich. He was trying to see who Jesus was, but on account of the crowd he could not, because he was short in stature. So he ran ahead and climbed a sycamore tree to see him, because he was going to pass that way. When Jesus came to the place, he looked up and said to him, "Zacchaeus, hurry and come down; for I must stay at your house today." So he hurried down and was happy to welcome him. All who saw it began to grumble and said, "He has gone to be the guest of one who is a sinner." Zacchaeus stood there and said to the Lord, "Look, half of my possessions, Lord, I will give to the poor; and if I have defrauded anyone of anything, I will pay back four times as much." Then Jesus said to him, "Today salvation has come to this house, because he too is a son of Abraham. For the Son of Man came to seek out and to save the lost."

Luke 19:1–10

"You have heard that it was said to those of ancient times, 'You shall not murder'; and 'whoever murders shall be liable to judgment.' But I say to you that if you are angry with a brother or sister, you will be liable to judgment; and if you insult a brother or sister, you will

be liable to the council; and if you say, 'You fool,' you will be liable to the hell of fire.

"You have heard that it was said, 'You shall not commit adultery.' But I say to you that everyone who looks at a woman with lust has already committed adultery with her in his heart."

Matthew 5:21–22, 27–28

Chapter 14

The moral principles of the Bible are supremely embodied in Jesus, who expresses those values both in his words and in his actions. Because Jesus is "the word made flesh" (John 1:14), his values are enacted in his life. This means that if we want to know how to treat other people, we need to look first and foremost at Jesus.

One of the primary features of Jesus' ministry is that he consistently welcomes people that others reject. Jesus welcomes the tax collector and all sorts of people decried by others as "sinners." He reaches to the outsider—the leper or the Gentile. He embraces the poor. The basic shape of his ministry involves bringing people who are on the margins into the center of God's grace.

For years, LGBTQ persons have been pushed to the margins of society, rejected and condemned by many. The example of Jesus gives clear instruction for how the church should now be treating them! Yet the church has often followed the model of the scribes and Pharisees—those pious believers in Jesus' day who looked down with judgment upon those they considered to be living wrongly.

Most churches today, noting the model of Jesus, would like to say that they welcome everyone. No church puts out a sign that says "You might not be welcome here." At the same time, churches will often note that while they welcome the *sinner*, they do not welcome the *sin*.

One could certainly observe in Jesus that while he welcomed people of all sorts, he did not affirm sin. In the story of Zacchaeus, Jesus reached out in fellowship to Zacchaeus, but he was not thereby approving all the times that Zacchaeus had defrauded people in their taxes! As Zacchaeus experienced Jesus' welcome, he did not see this welcome as an approval of his actions; he perceived it as an opportunity to change his ways. He promised to restore fourfold the amounts that he had cheated from others. Likewise in John chapter 5, when Jesus healed a man who was both physically and spiritually ill, he said to him in the end, "See, you have been made well. Do not sin any more." (John 5:14) The welcome of Jesus was not an acceptance of sin, but an opportunity for the sinner to experience redemption and renewal.

There are many churches that seek to apply this sort of "love the sinner, hate the sin" principle to LGBTQ persons. They insist that they warmly welcome LGBTQ people, even as they do not accept or approve "the practice of homosexuality." This is precisely the position embodied in the United Methodist *Discipline*. Churches that take this approach imagine that they are being authentically welcoming. Yet the vast majority of LGBTQ persons do not experience this attitude as welcoming at all. It is not because they do not see themselves as sinners. We are all sinners! It is because LGBTQ persons sense that churches are branding as sinful an essential part of who they are.

Zacchaeus' basic problem involved a lifestyle that he had *chosen*—he had chosen to exploit people by collecting taxes in a way that would enrich himself. In his encounter with Jesus, he was inspired to change his ways—to choose a lifestyle of fairness and generosity. This is how Jesus works with sinners generally. In our encounter with the grace of Christ, we are moved to change from one way of living to another. We cannot change things that are a part of our *nature*; Zacchaeus could not change his short stature! We change how we are choosing to live in our values and our treatment of other people.

Do LGBTQ persons choose their sexuality? For many years it was commonly thought that same-sex orientation involved in fact a personal choice—that people were in some sense choosing to go whatever route they were going in their sexual orientation—and that therefore they could choose to change their ways. Now it is well established that that sexual orientation is best understood as a trait, like other unchangeable personal traits such as height. Most churches today acknowledge this reality and affirm that *being* LGBTQ is not a sin.

At the same time, many churches still want to say that any *expression* of same-sex desire is a sin. They thus insist that while it is not immoral to have a same-sex orientation, it is a sin to *act* upon that orientation in a same-sex relationship. On this basis, they want to welcome the LGBTQ person while denouncing any practice of LGBTQ sexuality.

But is it possible to say that the *desire* for a same-sex relationship is not a sin, while the *practice* is a sin? In fact, this thinking runs completely aground upon the teaching of Jesus, who taught that there is no moral line between an inward desire and the corresponding outward action. Lustful desire for a person who is not one's spouse is a sin, right along with adultery. Hate toward another person is a sin, right along with murder. It was the Pharisees who wanted to define sin purely in terms of outward actions, but Jesus put the emphasis on the heart. As he said, "Out of the heart come evil intentions, murder, adultery, fornication, theft, false witness, slander." (Matthew 15:19)

When Christians therefore define all same-sex *practice* as sin, they are inherently defining all same-sex *desire* as sin. LGBTQ persons rightly perceive that they are being condemned when churches condemn "the practice of homosexuality." They know that what they feel in their heart is thereby denounced.

Further clarity is gained by considering the *change* that Jesus brings. The redemptive action of Jesus, in response to sin, always involves transformation of the heart along with a change in actions. Jesus not only drew Zacchaeus away from his behavior of defrauding his neighbors; he drew Zacchaeus out of the greed that had been motivating him, so that Zacchaeus no longer desired to enrich himself at the expense of others. We look to Jesus most of all to change our hearts, so that we no longer desire what is wrong.

If same-sex *behavior* is sin, then the change that we rightfully expect in LGBTQ people is that they no longer have any same-sex *desire*. But this is impossible, because same-sex attraction is precisely what defines a person as LGBTQ. It is therefore disingenuous to say to LGBTQ people that "we welcome you; we just condemn all same-sex practice," because that very attitude condemns them for who they are.

To move to a coherent sexual ethic, it is helpful to look at how churches view heterosexual desire. When a heterosexual person has a general desire for sexual intimacy, this is not a sin, because the desire for sexual intimacy was created by God, and what God creates is good. Sexual desire is something good as long as it is directed in accordance with God's will, who has called persons to express their sexuality in marriage, and indeed when it is so expressed it is celebrated! It is only the *misdirected* desire for sexual intimacy—intimacy with someone who is not one's spouse—that is condemned. When churches condemn adultery and fornication, heterosexuals do not feel that they are being condemned for being heterosexual, because the proper avenue for expressing their sexuality is honored and in fact blessed by God.

But when churches condemn *every* type of same-sex behavior, they are saying that the desire for same-sex intimacy is never good, since any expression of it would be sin. LGBTQ persons are unavoidably condemned. But how can the sexual desire that God has given to LGBTQ persons be something that is not good, and how can there be no proper avenue for it? The inconsistency here is resolved when a church affirms same-sex marriage, for then the same sexual morality is advocated for both heterosexuals and LGBTQ persons. This leads to a coherent sexual ethic, as noted in the chapter above.

LGBTQ persons continue in many parts of the church to be subjected to a message that there is something about them that is fundamentally unworthy. It is the kind of message that many people in Jesus' day heard from the Pharisees. But if the church is to genuinely follow the example of Jesus, it will actively welcome people who have been shoved to the margins. The nature of that welcome is further established with great clarity if we look at the working of the Holy Spirit—which will be the subject of the next two chapters.

The Church's Welcome

While Peter was still speaking, the Holy Spirit fell upon all who heard the word. The circumcised believers who had come with Peter were astounded that the gift of the Holy Spirit had been poured out even on the Gentiles, for they heard them speaking in tongues and extolling God. Then Peter said, "Can anyone withhold the water for baptizing these people who have received the Holy Spirit just as we have?" So he ordered them to be baptized in the name of Jesus Christ. Then they invited him to stay for several days.

Acts 10:44–48

Then certain individuals came down from Judea and were teaching the brothers, "Unless you are circumcised according to the custom of Moses, you cannot be saved." And after Paul and Barnabas had no small dissension and debate with them, Paul and Barnabas and some of the others were appointed to go up to Jerusalem to discuss this question with the apostles and the elders. So they were sent on their way by the church, and as they passed through both Phoenicia and Samaria, they reported the conversion of the Gentiles, and brought great joy to all the believers. When they came to Jerusalem, they were welcomed by the church and the apostles and the elders, and they reported all that God had done with them. But some believers who belonged to the sect of the Pharisees stood up and said, "It is necessary for them to be circumcised and ordered to keep the law of Moses."

The apostles and the elders met together to consider this matter. After there had been much debate, Peter stood up and said to them, "My brothers, you know that in the early days God made a choice among you, that I should be the one through whom the Gentiles would hear the message of the good news and become believers. And God, who knows the human heart, testified to them by giving them the Holy Spirit, just as he did to us; and in cleansing their hearts by faith he has made no distinction between them and us. Now therefore why are you putting God to the test by placing on the neck of the disciples a yoke that neither our ancestors nor we have been able to bear? On the contrary, we believe that we will be saved through the grace of the Lord Jesus, just as they will."

Acts 15:1–11

Chapter 15

As noted in the previous chapter, here is little debate among Christians about whether a congregation should welcome LGBTQ persons into the church. The question is whether LGBTQ persons are to be accepted *as they are*—their sexuality included—or whether LGBTQ persons are to be accepted with a *caveat*—they are acceptable only so long as they do not "practice their sexuality," that is, only if they repress their sexual identity. While some congregations are "open and affirming"—fully welcoming people who are in LGBTQ relationships—there are many others that accept LGBTQ persons only as long as they will abide by heterosexual rules, whereby sexuality is to be expressed only within heterosexual relationships.

There is a striking parallel to this situation in the book of Acts, which describes a major first century controversy involving Gentiles in the early church. The issue involved the conditions under which Gentiles could be welcomed into the church.

In the earliest years of the church, everyone in the church was Jewish. Christianity was a movement within Judaism, as people of Jewish faith accepted Jesus as the Messiah—the One who was the fulfillment of the Hebrew Scriptures. As the gospel spread, however, Gentiles began responding to the gospel message.

The term "Gentile" describes anyone who was not keeping the Jewish Law—all those Biblical instructions defining what a person can eat, how the Sabbath is to be observed, and so forth. By the first century, Jews had become scattered across the Roman Empire. As they met in synagogues, there were people who were not of Jewish background who became attracted to the Jewish faith, and who began to visit the synagogues. These persons, who were still Gentiles, became known as "God-fearers." Some of them took the major step of actually becoming Jewish—adopting the full Jewish Law—and they became "proselytes," people who were fully accepted and integrated into the Jewish community. Synagogues thus had a pattern by which Gentiles could become Jewish by committing themselves to follow the Jewish Law.

Early in the history of the church, churches formed that were separate from the synagogues. (Read the book of Acts, and you will see how the synagogue leaders quickly expelled those Jews who accepted Jesus as Messiah!) But even as distinctive Christian congregations formed, they were all people of Jewish background. They accepted Jesus as the Messiah, and they also continued to follow the whole Jewish Law. It was not long, however, before Gentiles became attracted to the Christian message, especially in response to the preaching of Paul and others.

A major question arose concerning the conditions under which those Gentiles could be accepted into the church. Most people in the churches felt that Gentiles needed to adopt the whole Jewish Law in order to be fully welcomed into the church. The Scriptures—which at this point consisted of the Old Testament books—mandated the Law, and there was nothing in those Scriptures indicating that the Law was not meant to be permanent. Christians did not believe that Jesus had invalidated the Law; to the contrary, Jesus had said, "I came not to abolish the Law but to fulfill it. Therefore whoever breaks one of the least of these commandments and teaches others to do the same will be called least in the kingdom of heaven." (Matthew 5:17,19). Based upon the clear teaching of the Scriptures and the words of Jesus, it seemed quite obvious to most early Christians that a person must obey the Jewish Law in order to be in good standing in the church.

But a few leaders in the church began to proclaim that the way God was working through Jesus was much bigger than the Old Testament law. They pointed out that ever since Abraham God had promised that through a descendant of Abraham the *whole world* would be saved. They argued that the Law was intended as a temporary guide for the Jewish people until the coming of the Messiah. Jesus certainly did not *abolish* the Law, but he *fulfilled* its demands by offering his life for humanity on the cross. This meant, these church leaders argued, that all people now can find salvation not by means of the Old Testament Law but through faith in Jesus Christ. The apostle Peter had gotten a vision from God precisely along this line; and the apostle Paul was vigorously proclaiming the message that Gentiles did not need to adopt the Jewish Law in order to follow Jesus as Savior.

There were thus two different sides in the church, who could not agree on the conditions for membership in the Christian community. One side said that Gentiles had to "become Jewish"—adopt the Jewish Law—in order to join the church. The other side said that Gentiles could accepted as they are—that the only qualification for acceptance into the church was faith in Jesus Christ. The situation was thus very similar to circumstances in the church today. In the current debate about human sexuality, one side says that LGBTQ persons must "become straight"—repress their own sexuality and adhere to the rules of heterosexual orientation—in order to be accepted in the church. The other side says that LGBTQ persons can be accepted as they are, that they should be fully welcomed without any requirements that they change, and that the only qualification for church membership is faith in Christ.

Both sides appeal to the Scriptures. But people have very different understandings of how to interpret the Scriptures! In the first century, a straightforward reading of Scripture seemed to favor the traditionalist side. The Law had been given by God to Moses, and God's people had been following the Law for over a thousand years. How could anyone say that the rules now were changing? On the other hand, some were arguing that the gospel shed new light on the old Law. How could the church resolve this disagreement?

Church leaders gathered for a council, which met at Jerusalem. The Jerusalem Council, described in Acts 15, is the model for church councils today, such as the United Methodist General Conference. It was a representative gathering of church leaders. But the Jerusalem Council made its final decision, not by taking vote in which delegates voted what they were already thinking, but by looking at *what the Holy Spirit was doing*.

Acts chapter 10 describes the story of Peter and Cornelius. Cornelius, a Roman centurion, was a God-fearer—one of those Gentiles who had developed interest in the faith of Israel but was still a Gentile. He had a heavenly vision prompting him to send for Peter, who, in the meantime, had his own famous vision in which God showed him that there is no longer any distinction between "clean" and "unclean" foods. Through this vision Peter got the message that there is no longer to be any division between Jews and Gentiles. Peter went thereafter to the home of Cornelius and preached the gospel; and the book of Acts reports what happened as follows: "While Peter was still speaking, the Holy Spirit fell upon all who heard the word. The circumcised believers who had come with Peter were astounded that the gift of the Holy Spirit had been poured out even on the Gentiles, for they heard them speaking in tongues and extolling God. Then Peter said, "Can anyone withhold the water for baptizing these people who have received the Holy Spirit just as we have?" (Acts 10:44–47)

The "circumcised believers" were of course Christians of Jewish background. They were "astounded that the gift of the Holy Spirit had been poured out even on the Gentiles." If the Holy Spirit was filling the Gentiles, this meant clearly that God was accepting the Gentiles—as they were! How did the believers know that the Holy Spirit was filling the Gentiles? They "heard them speaking in tongues and extolling God." The ecstatic "speaking in tongues" phenomenon was a particular sign of the presence of the Holy Spirit in the first century. In short, the early Christians saw that the

Holy Spirit was working powerfully in these Gentiles; and if God was accepting the Gentiles, the church needed to do the same! Peter baptized the whole group of Gentile believers into the church.

Later, at the Jerusalem Council, Peter referred to this and similar experiences, as he said, "And God, who knows the human heart, testified to them by giving them the Holy Spirit, just as he did to us; and in cleansing their hearts by faith he has made no distinction between them and us." (Acts 15:8–9) On this basis, the Jerusalem Council ruled that Gentiles were to be welcomed as they were into the church, without adopting Jewish Law. The Gentile believers were urged only to distance themselves from the most base features of paganism; as the book of Acts goes on to say, "We should write to them to abstain only from things polluted by idols and from fornication and from whatever has been strangled and from blood." (Acts 15:20)

It is highly significant to note how the church decided this whole controversy. There could have been endless arguments over the right interpretation of Scripture and tradition, just as there are endless arguments today concerning what the Bible says about human sexuality. But the church finally looked past such arguments by asking the central question, What is God doing? If God is filling these people with the Holy Spirit—moving them to faith and empowering them for discipleship—then God is obviously accepting them as they are. Case closed.

Look at LGBTQ persons who profess faith in Christ today and who are active in churches, and you will see the Holy Spirit powerfully at work. You will see a sincerity of faith, spiritual fervor, depth of commitment, and gifts of the Spirit that are just as strong in LGBTQ Christians as in heterosexual Christians. As Peter observed following his vision in Acts 10, "God shows no partiality." (Acts 10:34) If God is filling these persons with the Holy Spirit—which is clearly evident in countless cases—then this is the definitive sign that God is embracing these persons as they are. Can the church do anything else but follow God's lead?

Of course, accepting people into the church "as they are" does not mean that there are no moral expectations. In the first century, the Jewish Law in its particularities no longer applied; but all Christians were called to live a moral life and to distance themselves from the crassest features of the secular world. Christians are called to do the same today. First century believers were to "abstain from things polluted by idols," and believers today must likewise guard themselves against idolatry—that continual human tendency to make "gods" out of earthly desires and powers. First century believers were to avoid "fornication," and believers today must likewise stand firm against the temptation in our culture to fall into promiscuity. First century believers were called to have a respect for God's gift of life; modern believers must likewise stand firm against the world's propensity to fall into bloodshed. Surely LGBTQ Christians can follow such moral principles just as well as straight Christians!

The message of the Holy Spirit to the church today is clearly the same as it was in the first century. LGBTQ persons are to be accepted into the church as they are—on equal spiritual footing with everyone else—for the Holy Spirit is working in all, and we are all saved by the grace of Jesus Christ.

The Church's Outreach

Then an angel of the Lord said to Philip, "Get up and go toward the south to the road that goes down from Jerusalem to Gaza." (This is a wilderness road.) So he got up and went. Now there was an Ethiopian eunuch, a court official of the Candace, queen of the Ethiopians, in charge of her entire treasury. He had come to Jerusalem to worship and was returning home; seated in his chariot, he was reading the prophet Isaiah. Then the Spirit said to Philip, "Go over to this chariot and join it." So Philip ran up to it and heard him reading the prophet Isaiah. He asked, "Do you understand what you are reading?" He replied, "How can I, unless someone guides me?" And he invited Philip to get in and sit beside him. Now the passage of the scripture that he was reading was this: "Like a sheep he was led to the slaughter, and like a lamb silent before its shearer, so he does not open his mouth. In his humiliation justice was denied him. Who can describe his generation? For his life is taken away from the earth." The eunuch asked Philip, "About whom, may I ask you, does the prophet say this, about himself or about someone else?" Then Philip began to speak, and starting with this scripture, he proclaimed to him the good news about Jesus. As they were going along the road, they came to some water; and the eunuch said, "Look, here is water! What is to prevent me from being baptized?" He commanded the chariot to stop, and both of them, Philip and the eunuch, went down into the water, and Philip baptized him.

Acts 8:26–28

Chapter 16

Since the New Testament proclaims Jesus as Savior of the world, churches are impelled to take the gospel to everyone, to embrace everyone with the love of Christ. Is the church today ready to fully embrace LGBTQ persons? An extraordinary message in that regard is provided in the book of Acts.

The story involves an Ethiopian eunuch. The existence of eunuchs in the ancient world is related to the nature of royal households and governance. In the ancient near east, kings were in the pattern of having large harems. They also had many servants and government officials who spent a good deal of time in the palace, which was the seat of government. This created a potential problem — that the king's officers might start associating too closely with the king's harem! The solution to this was the eunuch.

A eunuch was a male who was castrated as a boy and thus destined to serve in a palace in the vicinity of the king's harem. The surgical procedure eliminated (or very sharply reduced) the sex drive. It also eliminated hormones which resulted in multiple other consequences as the boys matured. Eunuchs tended to have a more slender frame, no beard, and a voice that never got low; they were considered in the ancient world to be a kind of mix of male and female traits. But because eunuchs were considered "safe" to position in the center of the palace, they were often given significant roles in the royal court. Many eunuchs became quite powerful and influential, since they had the ear of the king or queen.

Eunuchs were broadly used in ancient near eastern kingdoms. There are records of eunuchs going all the way back to ancient Sumer in the 21st century B.C. But among the people of Israel, the whole practice was considered detestable, and there was a religious law against it. Deuteronomy 23:1 states, "No one whose testicles have been crushed shall enter the assembly of the Lord." This law provides the backdrop for the extraordinary story that is found in Acts chapter 8.

The book of Acts reports, "There was an Ethiopian eunuch, a court official of the Candace, queen of the Ethiopians, in charge of her entire treasury. He had come to Jerusalem to worship and was returning home; seated in his chariot, he was reading the prophet Isaiah." (Acts 8:27–28) The queen of the Ethiopians was not named Candace; *Candace* is a rendering of the Greek word, *Kandake* Κανδάκη, which was the official title of the queen of Ethiopia. This eunuch was obviously quite powerful, as he was in charge of her entire treasury. At the same time, he was a man of faith. The passage says that "he had come to Jerusalem to worship." He was obviously a Gentile, since there were no Jewish eunuchs; but he was clearly attracted to the faith of Israel. He was thus a *God-fearer* — one of those Gentiles who were attracted by Biblical faith, who were seeking to learn more and who often participated in synagogue worship, but who had not officially become Jews.

This man, however, would have been uniquely unwelcome in Jerusalem. Because he was a eunuch, he was forever banned from the temple. If he came to worship, it was to participate in festivals outside the temple or to visit other holy sites. It is notable that he persisted in his faith and his spiritual quest even in the face of that lack of welcome. His spiritual interest is illustrated in the fact that he was reading the book of Isaiah while he was traveling in his chariot.

Meanwhile, the book of Acts reports that an angel instructed Philip to go intercept this chariot on the road. This Philip is not the Philip who was a disciple, but rather an early church member who became very involved in church leadership and who is now known as Philip the Evangelist. (See Acts 6 for some of his story in the church.) What he was asked to do here was extraordinary.

Picture for a moment the man in the chariot, and imagine yourself to be an ordinary first century Judean Jew like Philip. The man in the chariot is African, so if you are a typical Jew in Galilee or Judea, he is of a different race. He is a Gentile, so he is not your religion. He works for a foreign government, so he is not a fellow citizen. And he is a *eunuch*. He is the closest thing in the New Testament to a transgendered person. His sexuality has been surgically altered. If you were a pious Jew from ancient Palestine, you would have multiple reasons to stay as far away from that chariot as you possibly could.

Philip is told to run the chariot down. He literally runs to catch the chariot (verse 30). Presumably the horse was going at a walk at this point or at most a slow trot! Then, upon invitation, he gets into the chariot (verse 31). Keep in mind that chariots were not very big. To get in meant that he would be snuggled right up next to this eunuch. Philip does not hesitate. He climbs into the chariot and begins to explain to the man, who had questions about what he had been reading from Isaiah, what it all meant. It was a passage about the suffering servant, which was fulfilled when Jesus offered his life for humanity on the cross. So, the book of Acts says, "Philip proclaimed to the eunuch the good news about Jesus." (Acts 8:35)

The eunuch comes, as a result, to faith in Christ. They pass some water, and the eunuch exclaims, "Look! Here is water! What is to prevent me from being baptized?" (Acts 8:37)

It is quite clear what could keep him from being baptized. There was a law in the book of Deuteronomy which says that *eunuchs are not allowed in the assembly of the faithful.* Baptism is initiation into the church; it is welcome into the assembly of the faithful. Based on clear Biblical law, it appears very plain that this eunuch should not be baptized and welcomed into the church. But he *is* baptized with full welcome by Philip, under God's instruction (verse 38).

There may have been a law in the Old Testament saying to keep such a man out; but the Holy Spirit obviously inspired Philip to bring this man in. Indeed this was not only a case of welcoming the man in. It was a case of seeking him out, chasing after him, leaping into his chariot, teaching him, and preaching to him in what is one of the most aggressive instances of evangelism in the entire New Testament, which is why Philip has subsequently been called Philip the Evangelist.

Every possible barrier — race, religious background, nationality, and sexuality — is overcome in this encounter. As Philip reaches to this man, it is a strikingly clear model for how the church is to relate to people who might historically have been excluded from the assembly of the faithful. God is calling the church to reach to everyone with the grace of Jesus Christ.

Laws in the Bible which appear to restrict God's welcome always have a particular historical context and an understandable function in that context. The law in Deuteronomy 23 was designed to keep the people of Israel from engaging in the practice of making people into eunuchs in the first place. The kings of Israel did have harems. King Solomon was said to have had 700 wives and 300 concubines. Obviously he was at a point where they just used round numbers! But there were no eunuchs in his court. Clearly, the law in Deuteronomy was successful. In other cultures, the many boys who were made into eunuchs had no choice in the matter. They were painfully forced into that destiny. But the Deuteronomy law prevented that injustice from unfolding in Israel.

In the book of Acts, however, there is an entirely different question. There was not a question of whether or not people ought to be eunuchs. There were already people who were eunuchs all over the ancient world; their particular sexuality was a given. The question for the church was how these people should be treated. The Spirit of God gave the clear answer — the law from Deuteronomy did not apply. In Christ all barriers are overcome, and there is no longer to be any placing of people into different categories, with some considered less godly than others. All are welcomed into the assembly of the faithful. As Paul would later put it, "There is neither Jew nor Greek, there is neither slave nor free, there is neither male nor female, for you are all one in Christ Jesus." (Gal. 3:28)

Moving Past Accommodation to Culture

Do not be conformed to this world, but be transformed by the renewing of your minds, so that you may discern what is the will of God—what is good and acceptable and perfect.

Romans 12:2

Chapter 17

One of the most common arguments against fully accepting LGBTQ persons into the church and approving same-sex marriage is that doing so would be an accommodation to the culture. The church, it is charged, would simply be giving in to the zeitgeist, changing its values to fit with the trends of the times. By sticking with "traditional values," so this argument goes, the church stands fast against such accommodation and refuses to be "conformed to this world."

But this argument fails to recognize where those "traditional values" come from. The traditional attitude toward same-sex relationships was itself shaped by a cultural heritage. Just as traditional attitudes towards African-Americans and toward women were shaped years ago by longstanding cultural patterns, so the traditional thinking about LGBTQ persons has been shaped by a long cultural history. For generations, people thought that the Bible called for a second-class social status for African-Americans and for women; they did not realize that they were reading the Bible through the lens of their culture. For centuries people have also considered the "homosexual lifestyle" to be unnatural and unacceptable; it is not surprising that people have believed the Bible to be supportive of those long-held views. But "accommodation to the culture" exists precisely here—in the insistence that Christians must hold to attitudes that the culture has held for generations.

"Do not be conformed to this world." Those words were spoke by the apostle Paul, one of the most revolutionary voices of the first century. He upended centuries-old attitudes toward Gentiles and spurred people to see God's word afresh, unshackled to the traditional ideas of the Sadducees and Pharisees. His words are by no means an admonition to stick with traditional thinking!

The church must not be conformed either to the ingrained ideas of the past or to trendy notions floating around in the present. Paul says rather: "Be transformed by the renewing of your minds, so that you may discern what is the will of God—what is good and acceptable and perfect." Surely this is God's call to Christians today: to be *transformed through the renewing of our minds*—which may very well mean thinking differently from how we have in the past!

How then do we "discern what is the will of God?" We can do so by moving past our culturally conditioned assumptions into a deep study of God's Word, so that, with God's help, we may "rightly explain God's Word of truth."

The Authority of Scripture

Make every effort to present yourself before God as one approved, a worker who has no need to be ashamed, rightly explaining the word of truth.
II Timothy 2:15

All Scripture is inspired by God and is useful for teaching, for reproof, for correction, and for training in righteousness, so that everyone who belongs to God may be proficient, equipped for every good work.
II Timothy 3:16–17

Chapter 18

This book has been grounded upon the conviction that the words of II Timothy are true—that the Bible is indeed the inspired Word of God, which provides the authoritative guidance for living.

When people argue for a traditionalist understanding of human sexuality, it is very common that they will claim that they are holding thereby to the "authority of Scripture." The implication is that those who hold to a "progressive" understanding are disregarding Scripture. But there are many people who take the Bible very seriously and who are led directly by the Bible to the conclusion that God is calling the church to fully accept LGBTQ persons. The dividing line between "traditionalists" and "progressives" on this issue is not over the authority of Scripture. It is over the question of how the Scripture is rightly understood.

People have differing opinions about how to interpret the Scriptures. It is good in the church to respect one another in those differences and not to assume that someone who thinks differently is disregarding Scripture. This however does not mean that one opinion is as good as another. When we believe in the authority of Scripture, we believe that God is speaking to us through the Scriptures, and therefore it is incumbent upon us, as imperfect as we may be, to "make every effort" to discern what God is truly saying!

Such effort requires far more than a cursory reading of passages or a search for opinions about the Bible that echo what we have always thought. If we truly take the Bible seriously, we must be ready, with open mind and heart, to study the Word in depth, using the best scholarly tools to understand language, context, and meaning. Only then do we start to get past our own opinions to hear the message of God.

The study of Scripture is much more than an academic enterprise. II Timothy 3:17 says that the practical purpose of the Scripture is that one may be "equipped for every good work." Our understanding of Scripture shapes how we as Christians finally engage the world. The church's stance on human sexuality is determining whether LGBTQ persons experience the church as a welcoming and accepting community or as a rejecting and condemning one. The church's stance is determining whether today's younger generations perceive the church to be a loving and positive force in the world or a judgmental and negative institution. The church's stance on this issue shapes how well the church can fulfill its mission; for the "good work" to which we are called is nothing less than reaching the world with the love and good news of Jesus Christ.

Epilogue

Some years ago I never would have imagined writing this book, especially because my thinking was the opposite of what has been expressed in these pages! I have always had a high view of the authority of Scripture; and based on my brief readings of the relevant passages, I felt that the traditional church stance was correct—that "the practice of homosexuality is incompatible with Christian teaching."

Then God changed my mind. It happened through Bible study, coupled with my observation of the Holy Spirit clearly at work in the lives of LGBTQ people in the church. I was moved to look again at the Bible and study the Word in much greater depth, drawing broadly on the extensive Biblical scholarship that has been done in recent years on the relevant passages.

"The word of God is living and active, sharper than any two-edged sword…" (Hebrews 4:12) God's Word continues to speak with power and can penetrate our hearts. As I looked afresh at the Scriptures, I was propelled to that "renewing of the mind" of which Paul had spoken. I began to come to the understanding that is expressed in the above chapters.

Still, I was not about to write a book on the subject. The book was precipitated by the crisis in the denomination where I have served as a pastor for more than forty years. As the United Methodist Church debated its stance, I heard people appeal to "the authority of Scripture" and make all sorts of claims about "what the Bible says"—claims which

I knew were well off the mark. I was moved to preach a sermon series on the subject, and then set about writing these pages.

My hope is that this book can contribute toward an understanding of what God's Word really says about a subject so painfully misunderstood. Very often people claim that the Bible requires a traditionalist understanding of human sexuality in which same-sex relationships are rejected. But every chapter above has come to the conclusion that the opposite is the case! Serious study of the Bible reveals that God's Word on human sexuality is not what people often think. The challenge of this age is for the church to hear clearly what God is saying.

> *Quotations from the Bible are from the New Revised Standard Version, unless otherwise indicated. Abbreviations:*
> NRSV *New Revised Standard Version*
> NIV *New International Version*
> KJV *King James Version*